MW01289743

How Sweet Was My Valley

Beside the flowing river,

The Little T

Sarah Simpson Bivens

A work of creative and historical fiction based on the true story of actual events. Some of the names used are fictitious while others are the actual names of the people who were active in the historic struggle. The cover painting is by the author.

Copyright © 2017 Sarah Simpson Bivens

All rights reserved

ISBN: 10: 1544003048
ISBN-13: 9781544003047

DEDICATION

To all those who loved the land
and the Little Tennessee River
and especially to those who tried to save it.
Also, to my friend and editorial advisor,
Brenda Lambert, who badgered me into writing this
very difficult story.

ABOUT THIS BOOK

Although this book is based on real life historical events, some of it contains composite fictional characters to express the attitudes often demonstrated during the long, heroic struggle to save the Little Tennessee River. For example, LaTisha Jamison and other fictitious characters from my previous novel *Crazy Creek* are also present and active in this book and make it, in part, a sequel to that earlier story. However, the rest of the book tells the factual events of many who fought the good fight for a good cause against all odds. Tish and her friends become part of the struggle.

The people trying to stop the Tellico Dam in order to save the beautiful, fertile valley and the river that ran through it were called the opponents or "The Resistors" and included numerous people of all ages and all walks of life. Some of them dropped out along the way, some died while still fighting, while others joined later towards the end.

This book is about and for the Resistors. It attempts to express the attitudes of some of them and does not attempt to hide their resentment and dislike of some real people who were proponents of the project during the struggle. Real names are used for many of the well-known individuals who were active in the fight. Because there were so many individuals over a long time span, it was impossible to give credit or blame to all, but some of the composite characters are meant to represent them.

ACKNOWLEDGMENTS

I wish to acknowledge the following sources which I found invaluable: the academic book *TVA and the Tellico Dam 1936 – 1979* by University of Tennessee history professors William Bruce Wheeler and Michael J. McDonald; the timeline provided by Zymunt Plater in the booklet, *Setting It Straight: a Thirtieth Anniversary Gathering . . . in Memory of the Little Tennessee River and Its Valley.* I was honored to have been invited to that reunion held November 14, 2009, in Vonore.

In November of 2017, it will have been an additional eight years since that reunion was held or a total of 38 years since the last of the landowners were evicted.

I acknowledge the information obtained from numerous newspaper articles, especially the *Cherokee One Feather*, North Carolina and the *Cherokee Advocate*, published in Oklahoma, from people who shared many stories, told and repeated, and from my own reporting published years ago in *Southline, A Magazine of the Country South.*

Zymunt Plater, the lead attorney who argued and won the environmental case before the U.S. Supreme Court, now a professor at the Boston College of Law, is the author of a non-fiction book *The Snail Darter and the Dam.*

The Law of Eminent Domain

The power of a government to take private property for public use without the owner's consent, providing just compensation is given.

American Heritage Dictionary

PROLOGUE

Who brought electricity to Tennessee Valley?

Although the Tennessee Valley Authority tends to imply that they alone brought electricity to the state, they did not. In fact, long before TVA was created, more than 45 privately owned companies were producing electricity in Tennessee. These private companies introduced water pumps, dairy equipment, and mining and woodworking tools, among other uses, all before the creation of TVA.

Soon after Thomas Edison founded the Edison Electric Light Company in 1878 and obtained various patents on generating electricity, industrious people all over the United States began the quest to generate and utilize electricity. In 1879 California Electric Company became the first to sell electricity to customers. In 1882, two more states began significant operations, Edison opened the first central power station in New York and Wisconsin became the site of the first hydroelectric station.

As early as 1905, entrepreneurs were creating electricity in Tennessee, paving the way for the state to become the site of the world's first multi-purpose lock and dam operation, the Hales Bar Dam on the Big Tennessee River in Marion County. Construction of the Hales Bar Dam began in 1913. At the time, the concept of hydroelectric energy was new. Since that project was privately owned, no citizens were evicted from their homes for its creation.

At about the same time, before 1916, The East Tennessee Light and Power Company constructed Ocoee 1 and 2, the twin hydro-electrical plants at Great Falls on the Caney River. The company also served portions of Virginia.

The state's largest private sector power company was the Tennessee Electric Power Company (TEPCO) which was formed in 1922 when the Chattanooga Railway and Light Company and the Chattanooga and Tennessee River Power Company merged. They then absorbed Toccoa Electric Power, Blue Ridge Corporation, Nashville Railway and Light, and Lookout Mountain, which were among the other 45 companies that combined.

Tennessee Power and Light, not TVA, was the company that first brought electricity to Loudon and the area around the valley of the Little T. It happened in the early 1900's. Perhaps some people who lived high in the mountains in isolated areas did not have access to electricity until later, but the promotional video created by TVA and WBIR's Heartland television series to celebrate the 80th anniversary of Norris Dam which shows an old fellow being thrilled by his first vision of a light bulb, is somewhat misleading about historical fact.

It was not until 1933, long after Tennessee was generating power, that TVA was created by Congress. Tennessee conservatives were against it, believing it was too much like communism, kin to nationalizing the energy sector. But, history has shown that people seem more tempted to try communism during economic downturns than at any other time. It was within the depression era when poverty occupied the thoughts of many Americans that citizens were willing to grant more power to the federal government. Hence, TVA was created promising prosperity. Privately, the first board members, according to their own historians, were more about social engineering. They decided they would force industrialization on the folks who lived along the river, whether they wanted it or not. They knew best; that's usually how people who favor big government feel. And, the people who feel empowered to make those decisions are members of government themselves, or, as one newspaper article described them, "beady-eyed bureaucrats."

People throughout the United States were impoverished at the time. The mountain people, though, did not suffer too much during the depression because they had always lived off the land; it was their way of life. These early settlers and their descendants, mainly Scotch Irish, chose to live in the mountains for various reasons, but primarily because of their desire for independence. When TVA personnel first interacted with Tennesseans, they noted that these people were happy in spite of being impoverished. These city-reared TVA employees said they simply could not understand how these rural people could be happy with little or no money to buy things. A certain distain for the values of these citizens seemed to continue through the following decades because the agency never seemed to care why people wanted to stay on their land.

As part of their self-promotion, TVA filmed people living in poverty in Tennessee and presented themselves as their savior. In an attempt to justify the first evictions of landowners, they posted signs which read "for the greater good". Never mind the fact that people were just as poor in other parts of the country as they were in the mountains and valleys of Tennessee. In the cities, poor folks had to line up outside the soup kitchens. In the rural areas, they went to their gardens and cellars, fished the streams. They survived without assistance, but TVA implied that these rural poor folks, hillbillies, were the ones who had to be rescued.

Although liberals in both political parties managed to get the agency created with strong emphasis on the word *Authority*, there remained existing power companies within the area. TVA and the federal government had their eye on the great and grand power of the Tennessee River but private-sector companies were already creating energy on it and its tributaries and these companies were an obstacle to TVA's plans to create government owned energy as well as social engineering. They began showing their political and bureaucratic importance by bullying TEPCO, forcing the power company to sue in defense of their business. In 1938, TEPCO sued TVA for trying to sell power to their customers in Nashville. In 1939, TVA won the lawsuit and as a consequence was able to buy TEPCO. That paved the way for TVA's taking of land along the rivers.

1
THE DREAM

LaTisha Jamison climbed into bed hoping she would have another night of peaceful sleep. Just as she switched off the lamp, the phone began ringing. Always alarmed by late night calls for fear of hearing bad news, she bolted upright as she fumbled for the light.

"Hello," she said, snatching the phone from its cradle on the bedside table.

"Tish, I hope I'm not calling too late." Her friend Julie said in a questioning voice.

"I was in bed but not asleep."

"I was just wondering if you and I could go visit Marlo's grave tomorrow since it will be exactly a year since she was murdered. What do you think?"

"I think that's a great idea," Tish said. "I had actually forgotten the date. Seems like most days run together now that I don't have a job."

"Are you sure you are up to it? I don't want to cause you to have any more of those terrible dreams like the nightmares you had after you were attacked."

"Don't worry, I'm much better now. Besides, I don't think anything in particular provokes them . . . they just come and go at random, but not nearly as much as they used to. Last night, I slept like a log through the entire night."

"That's great. So, shall we meet at the Valley Cafe and drive together to the Scott cemetery?"

"Yes, call me before you leave home and I'll meet you at the cafe," Tish said as she climbed back under the covers, once again hoping to sleep. Her little dog jumped into the bed and curled up next to her.

"There is something very special about you, Tyke," Tish said, remembering how the little Cairn terrier had tried to bite Alex's leg when he attacked her. It was a miracle that the vicious kick he had directed at the dog had missed Tyke, landing in the air, almost throwing him off balance. She really didn't know what Tyke had done next because while Alex was choking and beating her, she had lost consciousness. She reached down and stroked her faithful little friend and drifted to sleep.

Sometime in the middle of the night, she became aware that she was dreaming, somewhere in that twilight time, she thought, between wakefulness and sleep, because she was aware of having a dream. She was reliving an evening in 1964 when she, Julie, and Marlo had accompanied her parents to a meeting in Greenback, held in the school gymnasium. Then suddenly, they were in the auditorium of the Vonore school. Her dream seemed to switch locations but the meeting continued without interruption. There were lots of meetings in those days, various hearings about TVA's proposed plans to build a dam on the Little Tennessee River.

In her dream, she remembered her father talking while driving to the meeting. He was explaining to them that all of the farms and businesses located on the river and a number of communities in three counties, Loudon, Monroe, and Blount, were in danger if TVA went ahead with their plans. Her father encouraged the girls to become civic minded and understand the real threat to the area. They had agreed to go, somewhat half-heartedly, expecting to endure some long boring speeches, but that was not what happened.

The place was full of people, more than standing room only, with people filling the hallways and spilling outside, craning their necks and straining their ears, trying to know what was happening inside. Tish saw a man with red hair standing up front, promising the people new industries and many jobs. It was the TVA Chairman Aubrey "Red" Wagner and he was trying to sell the dam proposal to the crowd. Known to be an effective salesman, he had called the meeting, feeling rather confident that he could win support for the project.

Tish saw and heard it again, clearly, as if she were truly back in 1964. Wagner said, "We won't build it unless the people want it."

Apparently, Chairman Wagner wasn't counting on what happened next.

Judge Hicks of Monroe County quickly stood and

said, "All right, let's do a referendum."

The crowd, consisting primarily of farmers and landowners cheered and applauded enthusiastically. They were almost 100 per cent opposed to the dam.

Wagner, recognizing the fact that he was greatly outnumbered, said, "Well, the dam will impact more people than those of you who live here, so we couldn't do a referendum."

The crowd erupted in jeering and taunting; something he wasn't used to. Someone shouted loudly, "You said you wouldn't build it unless the people want it. We don't want it!"

This was followed by wild cheers and loud applause. Several members of the crowd were waving their arms, wanting to speak. The crowd became quiet, and one after another stood and stated numerous reasons why the dam was not needed and why they did not want to lose their homes and farms.

Tish could see them again clearly in her mind's eye. Most were dressed in the familiar casual attire of plaid shirts, jeans, and baseball caps, but some of the older men wore bib overalls. All of those who spoke gave solid reasons why they believed the farmland should be valued and saved. It was not simply how they made their living; it was a way of life here.

Several speakers pointed out that it wasn't easy to move a farming operation; even if one could find the land. It wasn't like moving from one house to another. And several had already been through it, having been chased off their farms in other places to make way for

Norris or Watts Bar or any one of the numerous other dams and lakes already in East Tennessee.

Most people were either hurt or angry; some had tears in their eyes. Others who did not farm nevertheless joined their neighbors, standing and reciting many solid reasons why the river and the valuable farmland should be saved. They brought up the rich history, the burial mounds, Fort Loudoun, and the special fishing afforded only by the free-flowing miles of the Little Tennessee River.

Tish tossed and turned, reliving the past in her dream state. Tyke jumped down and hit the floor loudly. Tish, having heard the thump made by Tyke as he landed, was wakened. Images and voices from the dream were fading quickly. The last words she could remember was someone whispering, "How sweet was my valley." It was only a murmur. She wondered why the dream-voice said *was* instead of *is*, because the valley was still there. TVA hadn't flooded it yet, although most people had given up hope of saving the river.

She turned over and tried to go back to sleep, saddened by the memories relived in the dream, but very thankful it was only a dream and not the panic-producing nightmare of the attack.

2
THE RIVER 1974

As she was driving to the Valley Café to meet Julie Smith for lunch, Tish Jamison noticed an increase in the number of vehicles with bumper stickers that read "Save the Little T" and still others that read "Don't bury my heart in the Little T". She was surprised because most folks had given up fighting the government and had come to accept the fact that their beloved river was doomed. The bumper stickers had been abundant and very visible throughout the 1960's when local residents had first organized the fight against the Tennessee Valley Authority and its plan to build yet another dam in East Tennessee. In fact, it was going to be the second dam built in Loudon County, only a stone's throw from the other one, the Fort Loudoun Dam. Some of the first bumper stickers remained on older trucks and cars, faded now by the years of passing time.

It was now 1974, a full decade since that first organizational meeting of the Association for the Preservation of the Little Tennessee River. In spite of the long odds, some opponents had never stopped fighting. Suddenly, she was shocked by the recollection of her dream. Maybe what the old mountain seer, Gertrude, had told her was true . . . perhaps she could pick up information or guidance through her subconscious mind if only she would meditate and listen. Some people call it instinct, Gertrude had said, and went on to explain that most folks were too busy to pay attention to guidance being offered.

There was something special about the Little Tennessee River. People could give a lot of varied reasons why they liked it and some of those reasons could also be said about other rivers, yet there was a difference, almost a reverence about the Little T as it rushed along in its free-flowing way. Psychics might say it was the special stored memories of all that had transpired in it and by it through so many eons, encompassing the lives and activities of the people who lived in the Overhill Cherokee capital of Chota, or in their other towns, Tanasi, Toqua, Tomatley, Citico, Maloquo, and Tuskegee.

Perhaps it was the spirits tied to the burial grounds of those ancient tribes, or maybe to the lingering voices of British soldiers who fought and died at Fort Loudoun. And later, during the Civil War, soldiers of both the North and the South tramped through the cornfields and some lived to tell of the richness of the harvest there before it was all plundered for their survival as they moved first this way and that, walking, riding the river, fighting.

Perhaps it was all that and more blowing in the wind, resting in gentle breezes and touching the heart-strings of people who could feel it. Actually, the river had been in danger for a very long time but not many people had known of the threat first made in cloistered backroom discussions where self-important individuals, both in and out of government, gathered to suggest various ways of social engineering using the manipulation of Tennessee's grand rivers. Because people who lived along the Little T didn't know what was in the minds of the politically well-connected, they had lived their busy lives beside the "strong water" as the Cherokees described it, farming its lush bottom lands of top soil which was more than a foot deep, building houses and barns and fences, and burying their dead in cemeteries next to the churches in communities nearby.

 Besides the hours people spent working in the fields or businesses along the river, some also spent time in it, swimming on hot summer days enjoying the cooling relief of the cold, clear current. Many traveled from other places to join the locals in a favorite past time – fishing for the special brown trout, abundant there. Still others just enjoyed floating down it.

Young boys did what Beryl Moser did when he was young; they chased their dogs through the fields and woodlands, sometimes walking slowly, hunting arrowheads and stones, especially near the banks and in the shallows. When farmers were plowing the fields, they sometimes spotted pieces of old earthen bowls and were reminded of the Cherokee who had lived there, wondering what it must have been like then. Most of the people who lived in the valley had no idea that the powerful government agency, the Tennessee Valley Authority (TVA), had put the well-loved Little Tennessee River on its list of 69 potential dam sites way back in l936. For many years after the agency was created, the Little T, as it was affectionately called, had been passed over as TVA proceeded to build other dams first. And, if anyone had heard about it having been put on a list of dam sites, they probably would have believed that too many other dams had already been built. Surely there would never be another one built here.

They were wrong, though. The reprieve ended when Aubrey "Red" Wagner, Chairman decided it was time for a new project. TVA had been lobbying for support since the '64 meeting of Tish's dream, but he waited patiently through the Eisenhower administration to request funding from Congress because he was well aware of the fact that Ike was not fond of the agency and had been quite open about his disapproval, thinking it was too much like the Communist Socialism – central government deciding what was best for the people. Also, as a matter of principle, Ike tended to be more tight-fisted than some when proposing his budgets. It was, after all, the taxpayers' money.

So Wagner waited until President Lyndon Johnson was in the White House before he pushed for funding for the Tellico Dam. Johnson gave him what he asked for by putting it in his budget.

When Tish pulled into a parking space at the Valley Café, she clicked off the ignition switch but continued to sit in her truck, experiencing more flashbacks of memory from the '60's and what people said about Red Wagner's thinking at the time. She realized that he had been right about the attitude of some local people who did not understand or appreciate the value of a stable farming community. Wagner had known that dam-building, the reason for TVA's very existence, had always been approved in the past, and he was sure it would be in the future. TVA supporters had used flood control as justification for previous dams, along with the need for hydro-power, but with all the dams already built on the Tennessee River, flood control was not really a believable reason. And, as for power, the trend was leaning more towards nuclear energy for the future and, besides that, there were already lots of dams generating power, including one already built in Loudon County. So, how did he and the agency plan to justify this new dam he was proposing? It would be for new industries and jobs, not merely make-work jobs for the thousands of TVA employees but to provide new, factory jobs for citizens who lived in the area. Wagner believed it would be an easy sell; that along with the promise of economic development. Never mind the fact that there were already plenty of lake-front properties already created by TVA on other lakes plus many acres of land in municipal parks created by various local governments and available for manufacturing plants in the area.

Unfortunately, Tish thought, Wagner was right about it being an easy sell to the politicians and he got funding from Congress rather easily with help from some in the media and other self-interested greedy souls who saw a way to profit at the expense of others.

Returning her thoughts to the present, Tish noticed Julie's car was already parked in front of the Valley Café, the only local restaurant still open after so many people had moved away. She climbed out of her truck and walked in, unaware of her somber expression. She spotted Julie waiting in a booth.

"Hi, are you late or am I early?" Julie said brightly. "Why are you looking so down? I hope there's no trouble between you and Neil."

"No," Tish sighed and smiled as she replied, "Everything is just fine with Neil. I was just thinking about the Little T. Those bumper stickers made me think about all the people who have moved away. I miss them. I just wish all of them had stayed to fight for their land. Wonder why there are so many new bumper stickers?"

"Oh, I guess you haven't heard the latest. Last week, on October 12, I believe it was, Hank Hill and Zyg Plater met with the remaining dam resistors over at Fort Loudoun and agreed to fight on in court, using the snail darter this time."

"Is there any hope of saving the river?" Tish asked, suddenly energized, "My Uncle Jack says, and I quote, 'the damn dam has been built, people have moved, just accept the inevitable.'" She sighed, shook her head sadly and said, "TVA built that dreaded structure back in 1967 but halted the project, saying they ran out of money and had to get more funding from the taxpayers before they could continue."

Julie responded, "One reason they keep running out of money is because they keep changing their taking-line. That's what they call it . . . the proposed boundary of the additional land that would border their new lake."

"I keep hearing about them wanting to take more and more land." Tish pushed her unruly walnut hair off of her face and grimaced.

"I'd say chances are slim to none of anyone being able to save the river now, but there is virtue in fighting for what we believe in, isn't there?" Julie asked.

"I think so, but I'm not sure. I know it's a sad thing to lose something you truly value." Tish shook her head, before continuing, "If I remember correctly, the only people who wanted the dam were individuals who saw an opportunity to make money one way or another, either directly from TVA or for publishing propaganda via advertising, or real estate transfers, or whatever else they could think of."

"One of the chief proponents is alleged to have known from the beginning exactly how he personally could and would benefit from the project: Mayor Charles Hall of Tellico Plains. Because he owns the telephone company there and knew the proposed lake would necessitate new telephone lines throughout the area and also knew how he could get the funds to do that, plus make himself major profits for the doing, he jumped on board with TVA right away. He would be able to apply and get a federal rural grant for the new lines and equipment. The grant would be for a million dollars, maybe more, I am told. And, the best part of getting a federal grant is because it doesn't have to be repaid! Most businesses have to take out a loan to expand their business and later repay it plus interest out of their future earnings, but not if you can get a government grant. It's free money!" Julie said.

Much like TVA's Chair, Aubrey Wagner, Hall was a pusher, a seller and a very prominent man in Monroe County. He reminded some folks of the Boss Hogg character in the "Dukes of Hazzard" television series because he was the big boss of Tellico Plains. The whole town seemed to be, willingly, under his control. Also, he was a Democrat and the Democrats were in the majority in Monroe County and in the Tennessee State Legislature at the time. He could influence them and they could influence everyone he needed on his side.

One thing was for sure, though, Judge Sue K. Hicks was a worthy opponent. Never mind the politics, Hall knew he was going to have opposition, but he would befriend TVA and lobby for them. The dam was going to be about 60 miles away but it was going to be named the Tellico Dam so that should publicize Tellico Plains and please his people. But, he didn't want to share his town with tourists so he was against promoting his town as a Gatlinburg-type place. He wanted to keep the area private, his very own town. His people could drive down the mountain, 60 miles to work. He could almost taste the victory and was very open, glad to share his views with just about anybody at any time. Both Julie and Tish knew all about the struggle that had been going on for a decade. They sat in silence for a few minutes, looking at the menu although they had it memorized. Finally, Tish said, "TVA found out at that first meeting that they were not going to build the dam without a fight, but they had never had a fight quite like this one. Hopefully, they'll think twice before trying to fund anymore dams."

"They'll have to start damming creeks because there won't be any rivers left," Julie said.

"There's still the Tellico River. Wonder what they'd name that dam if they built one there!" Tish said as she and Julie began laughing. It had always irked folks that the dam on the Little Tennessee was going to bear the name of a mountain town and river that was approximately 60 miles away. Many lost sight of the fact that Tellico was originally a Cherokee word, translated by one Cherokee old-timer to mean "Big Money."

"Perhaps our continued fight will shed a little light on TVA's questionable practices which some landowners call lies and deception. TVA has succeeded over and over with their talk of "sacrificing for the greater good." Time and time again, good people have lost everything without seeing any of the alleged greater good."

"Although neither one of us has come out and said it," Julie said with a twinkle in her eye and a shake of her auburn hair, "all this reminiscing is preparing us to go help fight for what's probably a lost cause. I hope I don't lose my job." She sighed.

"You know, some in the courthouse crowd where I work practically worship TVA. Guess I should remember that Davey Crockett was slain at the Alamo, fighting for a lost cause."

"Well, I don't have a job and I may never find another one, but I'm still going to do whatever I can do to help if it's nothing more than writing letters to congress and the newspapers." Tish said. "Did I tell you I dreamed about all this last night? You remember that meeting we went to over in Greenback with my parents?"

"Yes," Julie said.

"Well, that was in my dream. I couldn't imagine why I dreamed about something that happened 10 years ago, but now I know why. All these new bumper stickers have made me realize why I had that dream."

"Wow!" Julie exclaimed, "You've got it, whatever *it* is – that same thing that Gertrude has."

"No, I'm not like Gertrude. She can see into the future. I can't do that. Sometimes I happen to pick up on things in the present, that's all. Everyone has intuition."

It had been a little over a year since Tish was brutally attacked by the man who had murdered her dear friend, Marlo Scott. Only recently had she begun to feel whole again. It had taken even longer for her to stop having the nightmares she had continued to have for months following the terrible assault which almost claimed her life. She was both physically and mentally unable to keep her job as a social worker due to the broken ribs and other injuries plus the emotional trauma she had suffered during the attack. As for the job she held at the time, the attacker had been her boss in the Department of Human Services forcing a shake-up of the entire agency after Alex Morgan was arrested.

While she was healing, she had felt pampered by her many friends, especially Neil Darren who along with her father had saved her life. As soon as she was able, she had kept busy helping with chores around her parents' farm where she stayed during her initial recuperation after being discharged from the hospital. A couple of months later, she had returned to her nearby cottage and was trying to resume her old life. Neil Darron had been eager to keep her busy as well.

Roger Kinealy approached the booth and greeted Tish and Julie, "Hello, you two fine looking ladies. What brings you out into the world with the rest of us regular folks?"

Both women smiled and Julie said, "We can always depend on you to make a girl feel better." Julie said.

Tish recalled the days in Jr. High when Roger and his friends had embarrassed her by singing a jingle they had made up: "Tish, Tish, what a dish," this was followed by a long whistle." She could laugh about it now, but it wasn't funny then.

"How are you these days, Roger? We're here re-hashing the saga of the Tellico Dam."

"Scoot over," Roger said, inviting himself to sit down. "I just heard about the effort to stop the thing. It continues to amaze me that so many diverse groups came together to try to save the river and still couldn't get it done. Who would have thought that a whole bunch of Democrats and Republicans, the Sierra Club, Cherokees, farmers, archeologists, fisherman, histori-ans, timber people all opposed the thing and came to-gether to try to save the river."

"And, don't forget the area industries, especially the creameries who process milk from the dairy farms and Goldkist who built the grain elevator and bought soy-beans, corn, wheat and oats from the row-crop farmers and still others, especially the agricultural interests who came together to oppose the project." Julie com-mented.

"I know," Tish said, "and don't forget about the tree nursery at Rose Island where millions of pine seedlings are grown for the Hiwassee Land Company and shipped to Georgia, Alabama, Mississippi and elsewhere in Tennessee. These seedlings are important to Bowaters, the giant British industry that makes pa-per from pulpwood. And, of course, all the fishing and boating businesses, where people rent boats and buy bait, plus the restaurants and cabin rentals were, and some still are, along the river. I don't think everyone realizes just how much people seem to love fishing the Little T or how many fisherman there are, not just folks from around here. They come here from everywhere."

"And what a line-up of significant individuals have been here." Roger added, "Remember when Justice William O. Douglas visited the area, along with his wife?"

"Yes. It was rather exciting to learn that such a revered man was on our side. It's interesting to me that he was the first Supreme Court Justice, I believe, to give voice to the environment and perhaps prepare the way for it to have legal standing. He was appointed by President Roosevelt, a Democrat, but it was President Nixon, a Republican, who created the Environmental Protection Agency. So neither political party can take all the credit for trying to save the environment or all the blame for trying to kill the river," Julie said.

Tish nodded in agreement.

"One of the men who got the most publicity besides Justice Douglas was Judge Sue K. Hicks from Madisonville because of that song 'A Boy Named Sue' that Johnny Cash made famous when he recorded it in San Quentin. Judge Hicks showed me the two signed albums that Johnny Cash sent to him. In addition to his signature, Cash also wrote a lyric from the song, 'How do you do,' on one of them." Roger said, then continued, "It's interesting how all that happened. The songwriter, Shel Silvestein, was at an event over in Gatlinburg where Judge Hicks was the guest speaker, and when he was introduced, Silvestein got the idea for the song and later played it for Cash.'" They all smiled remembering the oft-told story.

"Too bad none of the media included Hicks opposition to the dam when they wrote all those articles about the man behind the song. That might have helped raise awareness outside the area." Roger added, as he looked at his watch, then said,

"Wish I could stay longer, but I've got to go. Good to see both of you." Slowly, he unwound his long frame from the booth, stood up and winked with a big smile that dimpled tan cheeks in his face, "As you know, I'm still single and available. Give me a call and we'll go party some time."

"You know perfectly well that I'm not single," Julie laughed as they watched Roger walk to the counter. In high school, Julie was one of many girls that Roger had dated.

"That guy is never going to grow up and settle down . . . forever the flirt," Tish said, "but he was against the dam and I assume, by the way he talks, he still is; we can assume he has a serious side."

"Judge Hicks was there at that first meeting to organize the Association to Save the Little Tennessee River, along with Judge Ben B. Simpson of Loudon. Both of the lawyers knew the condemnation of land and the impoundment was going to be bad for the local governments as well as for the river and landowners." Tish recalled. "And like Roger said, it was a bipartisan gathering. Simpson was a Republican and

Hicks, a Democrat, and together they did the legal set-up of the organization."

"It's impossible to be stay depressed around Roger. He's what Pa would call a 'card'," Julie said. They got a refill of coffee, and continued their discussion, deep in remembered thoughts.

"Yes," Julie sighed, "Some folks, including Jean Ritchey, Mr. Lackey, Beryl Moser, Alfred Davis, and so many others went to Washington and tried their best to get members of Congress to save the river and the land." Julie paused, staring at nothing, seeing memories instead. "In the end, I think it was a numbers game. More citizens eventually believed the propaganda spouted by TVA than those of us who didn't, and the politicians supported the majority. At least, that's what I think," Julie said, then added, "or perhaps it was just plain greed. Maybe they could see the facts but chose to ignore them, hoping to personally benefit, not giving a thought to those who would suffer the loss of their homes and livelihoods."

"Well, one thing is for sure," Tish lamented, "TVA is certainly a slick bunch. They got Tennessee's Governor Clement on board before the public even knew any details. He's one of the Democrat bad guys in my book. The only governor that has tried to help is Republican Winfield Dunn and term limits won't allow him to run again. He asked TVA to stop the project, but they just ignored him. And right now, we've got Gov. Blanton, another Democrat, who is known to be a big TVA supporter, also suspected of being a crook."

"And, at some point, I heard that TVA got the *Knoxville News Sentinel* to promise not to publish any anti-dam sentiment, at least that's what Sam Venable, that popular columnist, told some of the opponents. TVA bought ads, not to mention their huge workforce. I imagine all or at least most of their employees bought newspapers and were also voters. Only the *Knoxville Journal* printed both sides, including the real facts expressed by the opponents. As the years went by, there were some changes in the newspapers, I think the *Sentinel* started publishing letters, but I'm not sure. But, I think it's too late now to stop them. TVA is just too powerful." Julie said.

"You are probably right, and Uncle Jack is probably right too, but I hope Hank and Zyg can win." Tish sighed, "I know the fight will cost money. It costs money to file any kind of lawsuit and go to court. How are they going to raise the money or do you know?"

"I understand that Asa McCall passed his hat at the meeting. You can ask your father. He went with Pa. That's how I heard about it, from talking to Pa. You can bet the newspapers will be blasting away at the poor old landowners, accusing them of standing in the way of progress."

"I have come to despise that word, *progress*," Tish frowned, "seems like it is used to represent everything I'm against and nothing I'm for.

"I will talk to my father and see if there is anything I can do to help but I don't have a clue what that would be." Tish sighed, paused, before adding, "but what about our reasons for meeting today? I know the weather is not as warm as usual for this time of year, but it's stopped raining, so are we still going out to the cemetery to visit Marlo's grave? It's hard to believe that it's been a year since she was murdered."

"Yes, I think we should. We were her very best friends. Do you think departed souls know when people visit their graves?" Julie asked.

"No . . . I have no idea, but *we* will know and our going will make us feel better, even if Marlo doesn't know we're there." Tish said.

3
THE LETTER

It was a cold blustery day in Boston when she left her mother's bedside in Boston General Hospital. She had dutifully telephoned her mother's attorney, as requested, but for the life of her, she did not know why her mother had insisted she do so.

"Can't it wait, Mother? I'd rather stay here with you than go sit in some lawyer's office." Katherine knew her mother did not have much time left in the world and didn't think she should leave her.

"Katherine, promise me you will keep the appointment. If you don't, I'll have one of the nurses call him and have him come here. Before I die and meet my Maker, I have to know that you know certain things."

Cynthia looked at her daughter with pleading eyes and finally relief as Katherine shrugged assent and left the room. Thank goodness, she thought, my brain is still working. The tumor hasn't made me forget what needs to be done. I've just got to hang on long enough to know it's done.

The attorney's office was only a city block away from the hospital so Katherine decided to walk, thinking that would be quicker than getting the car out of the lot and finding another place to park. Maybe moving would help relieve some of the tension she was feeling. The keen wind felt good on her face as she walked briskly, barely seeing her surroundings, curious yet eager to get the meeting over with so she could return to the hospital.

An elderly statesman-like gentleman with gray temples ushered her into his office as soon as she arrived. "I'm Jim Johnson," he said. "I've known your mother for years and I'm just as curious as you are about what is in this document she asked me to keep for you. She told me not to read it until either her death or at her request and I have honored her wishes." He opened the document and began reading:

In 1944, when I went into labor, I was in Ashville where I was living and working. As you know, my husband was killed in combat not long after I found out that I was pregnant. I was devastated but comforted by the fact that I was carrying his baby. Anyway, on that same December day, another woman also went into labor and was admitted to the hospital. It would have been a typical kind of day at the hospital except for the fact that they had been having a dispute about wages and quite a number of nurses had called in sick. The hospital had several new substitute nurses on duty that night at the time we finally had our babies. It turns out that the other lady had delivered premature twins only minutes before my baby was born. There was a lot of rushing around as the staff took care of both of us mothers and the three babies which were lined up in the nursery where they keep infants. All three babies were tiny. I don't know what the odds were of three premature babies arriving at the same time but that's what happened. One nurse said it was because the moon was three-quarters; no doubt, an old wives tale.

I heard later that night that one of the twins had died. Although the parents were saddened by that news, they were so thankful that the other baby seemed to be thriving, they didn't really grieve. They were an older couple and had pretty much given up having children. I heard a nurse making arrangements to have the infant's body transported to a Funeral Home in Vonore, Tennessee, for burial in a cemetery near there, in Jensen's Valley.

Anyway, all was well with you, except you did cry a lot. I was discharged and everything was fine with us for several years. It was not until you were almost six years old and about to start school that I realized what must have happened. I was reading the newspaper there in Ashville when I saw a photograph of a couple with a child that looked exactly like you. The paper identified the couple as being Ralph and Gloria Scott of Jensen's Valley, Tennessee. They were guests of someone over at the Biltmore place. Then it hit me that the photograph was of the woman who gave birth on the same night that I did! I never did hear the last name while I was in the hospital, but I did hear her given name. Her husband kept saying, 'Gloria, it's going to be all right,' over and over, he said it. From conversation with the nurses, I understood that she had planned to have her baby in Tennessee where they lived but since she went into labor early, she went to the Ashville hospital.

I was in shock. I tried to convince myself that it was just a coincidence that the little girl in the photo looked like you, but deep down, I knew the child was your twin and that my baby was the baby that died. Because I didn't purposely take someone else's baby home . . . it really was the hospital's fault . . . I didn't know what I was supposed to do. I loved you so much. After all, I believed you were my own biological daughter for all those years. And you still are my daughter like you would have been if you were adopted. I was torn between going to the Scotts and telling them about the mistake or keeping it to myself. In the end, I was too afraid of losing you to take the risk so I just tried to forget it. But, because the Scotts were socialites, I saw their picture again not too long after the first time. I figured sooner or later, someone would see that you and their daughter were identical. That's when I decided to move. I was an excellent secretary so I went to one of those agencies and got a job as far away as I could move. I had never remarried, so there was no one to argue against my decision except my parents. They didn't want me to move away but they had other children and grandchildren so I wasn't worried about them. That's why and when we moved up here to Boston.

Now that I am dying, I want you to know who your birth parents are. Unfortunately, you will never get to meet your twin. Her name was Marlo and she was murdered last year. I have managed to keep up with the Scott family through the various newspapers in North Carolina and Tennessee. I'm sure all of this will be a shock to them as it must

*be to you, but I have to set things as right as I can. I love you
so very, very much and, please remember that I am a victim
as much as you are in this mistake. But, it would have been
far worse for me had I been told the truth at that time and
had to leave the hospital without a baby. I was still grieving
over my husband and you were the only reason I had for living.*

Please forgive me for not telling you sooner.
Signed,
Cynthia Martin

The attorney and Katherine stared at each other for
several minutes before either of them spoke. Mr. Johnson then addressed Katherine softly, "Take your time
getting used to this news. I know your mother is very
sick…"

Katherine nodded. Then she said, "What am I supposed to do? This is surreal."

"If I were you I'd continue living as you have been
as Katherine Martin, at least for now. I understand you
have taken a leave of absence from your job to be with
your mother. And, Katherine, for all practical purpos-
es, she is your mother. She loves you, she reared you,
just as if she were your biological mother or an adop-
tive one. Later, I will help you contact the Scotts if you
wish to fulfill your mother's request, perhaps through
their attorney. If the Scotts are wealthy, they might
suspect that you are trying to scam them for money
since they lost their other daughter, but I know your
mother and I am certain she is telling the truth. She

wrote this when she was in sound mind 10 years ago."

Katherine shook the attorney's hand and said, "Thank you for your advice. I'll be in touch. Right now, I need to go reassure Mother." She was shaking, uncertain how she should feel about the letter.

After she left the building and began walking to the parking lot, she spotted a bar and decided she needed a drink very badly. She ducked in and ordered a Vodka Collins. Her mother thought she drank too much so she abstained most of the time, but the information she had just learned shook her to the core and shouted for a drink.

As Katherine sat staring into the tall glass, she was oblivious to the many admiring glances cast her way by those gathered in the bar. She was in her prime, an exceptionally beautiful young woman with tawny blond locks falling from the clasp which held her hair away from her face. She was wearing brown slacks and a pull-over sweater, and very little make-up.

One young man decided to approach her. He knew who she was, but he couldn't remember how.

"Hello, Miss Martin, do you remember me? My name is Victor Ashton. I'm an attorney in the building next door."

Katherine turned to face him. "I'm sorry, but I'm afraid I don't recognize you. Perhaps you saw me in court; I cover a lot of trials for the *Boston Globe*. And, most folks call me Kat."

"That's probably it, then." Victor said, but his attempt to continue a conversation failed as Kat rose quickly from the stool, turned and walked briskly from the bar.

4
CHANGES

The temperature was dropping quickly and Kat could surmise that as she looked from the hospital window at people hurrying and clasping themselves on the street below. Now, most of them were wearing coats when earlier, she had seen people walking leisurely, clad only in jackets or sweaters.

October is just too early for winter, she thought. Although her mother had reared her mostly in the North, she had never liked cold weather and always wanted autumn to last longer than expected, but it rarely did. She turned again to look at this woman who had reared her and couldn't help wondering what her biological mother looked like. And, what had her twin looked like before she was killed. She would find out soon because she planned to go there from Ashville where she was going for the funeral and final resting place for Cynthia Martin. Pre-arrangements had already been made. Cynthia had thought of everything.

She sat on the bed and watched. Cynthia was in a deep sleep and not expected to last through the night.

She wished there was a relative she could call, but none lived close by.

She moved to the chair and dozed for a while until she was awakened by the sound of the monitoring machine which was sounding an alarm. Nurses rushed in followed by the doctor. Cynthia was gone. Although Katherine thought she would be through with her tears, she was not. They continued to flow as one of the caring nurses gave her a shoulder to cry on. The staff had noticed that Katherine was always there alone. It was not that uncommon in the city, yet there were usually friends if not family coming in and out of the building when patients were waiting for death to take them.

There was not much left for Katherine to do now, except go home and pack for the trip. The nurses had phoned the local undertaker who was making arrangements for the transportation of Cynthia's body to a funeral home in Ashville.

Kat's activities were a blur during the next few days as she made reservations in a hotel in Ashville and purchased a plane ticket. Cynthia had left the names and phone numbers of a few people for her to contact. Kat wasn't close to anyone there because, when Cynthia moved, she broke ties with almost everyone back home, all to protect the identity of her little girl.

The service itself was simple but fitting for a good person who meant no harm to anyone. She was laid to rest in a plot next to her late husband whose body had been recovered from the battlefield in Europe and returned for burial in Ashville.

Following the service, Kat sat through a meal arranged by the church and attended by some of Cynthia's surviving relatives and old friends. Her own Boston accent, markedly different from the Carolinians, made them laugh at her and she, them, as they compared the dialect of various expressions.

Finally, she was able to return to her hotel room where she was at last able to rest. She had not slept as long and as deep in months. Although she still felt the stress of the situation, the loss of someone she truly loved, the shock of knowing she had a different biological family, all of it, weighing heavily on her mind, yet, she somehow felt like part of a puzzle had been solved. For her entire life, she had felt somehow separate, like a part of her was missing. Then, about a year ago, she felt a sudden anguish which made no sense. She had wondered if she was going crazy, becoming mentally ill because she cried and cried for no apparent reason. The sadness passed, yet, that feeling of separation continued. And now, that emptiness was gone. She felt whole for the first time ever in her life. And, that made no sense at all, for she was absolutely alone except for a few not-so-close friends back in Boston. Tomorrow, she would head to Jensen's Valley to find out more about her biological parents.

The next morning when Kat woke from her deep sleep, she felt renewed and ready for the challenge that faced her. Jim Johnson had found out the name of the Scott's attorney and forwarded a copy of the letter to him. She had made an appointment to meet with him and wondered what she should expect. Skepticism, probably.

Now, she finally understood why her mother had not taken her there for visits or vacation. When she saw the attorney in Jensen's Valley, she hoped she would find out when and how or even if she could meet her biological family and also, find out as much as she could about her deceased twin.

She wasn't sure how long it would take her to drive her rental car to Jensen's Valley since it wasn't even on the map. She only knew that it was a community close to Vonore in the foothills of the Smokies, so she left Ashville early and drove slowly, admiring the rich colors of autumn that were vibrant here when all the leaves in Boston had already turned brown and fallen. She did know quite a bit about the Ashville area from stories her mother had told her and had wanted to visit but her mother had always made excuses as to why that wouldn't be a good idea. Although she had grown up in the city, she didn't feel that she belonged there. There was somehow a tug on her to get away. She liked the feel of small towns and the rural countryside. As soon as she was old enough, Kat had taken waitressing jobs in Nantucket during the summers to get out of the city. Nantucket was a busy tourist place, but it maintained a feeling of history with its cobblestoned streets and roof-top widow-walks that still existed on some of the old houses once occupied by seafaring families so many years ago. She was able to ride her bicycle to work at Captain Toby's Chowder House, not far from the wharf. And, in the evenings, she enjoyed the sounds of chatter as visitors gathered on the main street.

It was still early when she packed her bag and put it in the rental car. She hoped to find a different place to stay, a nice but less expensive motel or hotel. Perhaps even a B & B somewhere closer to Jensen's Valley.

She drove to the take-out window of a Hardee's Restaurant and ordered a sausage biscuit and coffee, then continued driving until she spotted a small roadside park. She pulled up beside a concrete table and bench where she sat down and enjoyed her breakfast in the company of a chattering squirrel who seemed to believe she had come for the nuts dropping from the walnut tree he had claimed for his or her own. Before getting back into the car, she walked about the small area, stretching her legs. The small park was well positioned in a cluster of trees clad with vibrant-colored autumn leaves. Across the road was a pleasant view of cattle quietly grazing in a fading green pasture.

It was almost noon when she arrived in Jensen's Valley but too early for her appointment so she decided she would go to the cemetery where her twin was buried. She had obtained the directions to that cemetery from Charles Jamison, the Scotts' attorney. She was able to drive straight to it without difficulty. After parking by the gate, she got out and walked through the well-tended and scenic setting, reading the grave stones as she walked. She found the headstone for Marlo Scott and a small one beside it which read simply, "Infant twin daughter of Ralph and Gloria Scott, sister of Marlo." It gave the dates of birth as December

10, 1944. There was no date of death for the infant.

Kat felt strangely at peace, standing there by the graves. She bowed her head and was reciting a prayer when she heard the sound of an automobile approaching. So familiar with the sound of vehicles in the city, she was oblivious to the sound of people getting out of the car that had stopped by the gate to the cemetery.

As they approached, Julie remarked to Tish, "Wonder who that is . . . all I can see is the back of her head. It's not Gloria though or Margaret. She's blonde so maybe it's some of their kinfolks."

"Well, let's go see." Tish chimed, getting out and slamming the door shut.

Julie and Tish walked carefully, watching where they stepped because a recent rainstorm had left little pools of water at intervals along the walkway. As they approached Marlo's grave, the unknown figure standing there turned to face them.

Julie let out a terrified shriek and fainted, falling hard and fast, landing beside an awe-struck Tish who seemed to be frozen in place. Tish was assuming, as Julie must have, that Marlo's ghost was standing before them.

Kat rushed over to see if the woman on the ground needed some kind of assistance. Since Tish was staring blankly, Kat bent over Julie who was murmuring something with her eyes still closed. "Are you all right, Miss? Did you fall? Should I call an ambulance?" Kat asked.

Tish tried to regain her senses, but remained in shock. This ghost was acting like a regular live person.

"Marlo," she muttered, but didn't know what else to say.

"No," Kat said, understanding now what had happened. "I'm not Marlo, I'm her twin."

"But, you're grown up. Her twin was a baby." Tish was still confused.

"Look, I'm so sorry about this," she looked down again at Julie who was trying to sit up. "I'm not a ghost or a spirit. I'm a real person. They got the babies mixed up. I'm Marlo's twin, not the baby buried there. I just found out myself. I would explain more but I have an appointment with an attorney. Looks like I'm going to be late," Kat said glancing at her watch. "Do you happen to know where Charles Jamison's office is?"

"Yes, he's my father." Tish stammered. "If you want to follow us, we'll show you the way."

Tish and Julie drove in silence, still awed by the resemblance of the stranger to their old friend. They were also feeling a little embarrassed because both had believed her to be a ghost. The sound of a horn honking from a passing car brought them to attention.

"Who was that?" Julie asked.

"Beryl Moser," Tish said. "I'll bet he was at that meeting of the landowners. He's one that has never given up or given in to TVA or the pleas of the greedy folks who have figured out a way to make a dollar out of this fiasco."

"You mean people like Charles Hall who owns the phone company and has supposedly gotten rich from big government grants to upgrade his system?" Julie asked.

"That's what people say. He's definitely influential in Monroe County. Personally, I don't know the man, He jumped on the dam-wagon from the get go; I'm surprised they didn't name it the Hall Dam."

Tish glanced into her rearview mirror to make sure Kat was still following her before turning off of Niles Ferry Road.

5
REUNITED

Tish continued driving in silence until they were close to the law office which was located near the diner where they had eaten earlier in the day.

"I always knew identical twins looked alike but never this much. I really thought it was Marlo standing there." Julie said.

"Me too," Tish echoed. They parked and waited for Kat to accompany them to the office. As they entered, Tish remarked to the secretary, "Better brace yourself, this young lady is not Marlo."

Judy gasped as she was introduced to Katherine. "Go right in," she motioned, "he's expecting you."

"If you don't mind, we'll just wait out here." Julie said, "We need to find out what's going on. It's just amazing how much alike they are, isn't it? Although Kat sounds sort of like a Yankee, the tone of her voice is just like Marlo's."

Judy shook her head, "It's remarkable."

"What do you know about her?" Tish asked the bewildered secretary.

"All I know," Judy said, "is that she made an appointment to see your dad following a letter he got in the mail and a phone call from some attorney up north."

The door opened and Charles stuck his head out, "Why don't you girls come on in here. You might be some help with what we need to do."

Julie and Tish leaped to their feet and hurried into the office.

"I understand you three have already met. Sorry it was at the cemetery. I would have told you about Kat but I wanted to meet her first myself to see if I concurred with Jim Johnson's assurances that she was truly the Scotts' daughter. Now that I have met her, I certainly do, so we have to arrange for Ralph and Gloria to meet her. I know seeing her for the first time is going to be a shock since it will be just like seeing Marlo again. I think it would be better for the Scotts to come here instead of having Kat go to Florida. It would also be less costly for this young lady, what do you think? Then, you two could go with her out there to the Scott mansion to meet them. Would that work, do you think?"

"Yes, I think so. Have they been back since the funeral last year?"

"No, they haven't been back and they haven't done a thing. Although the Hobsons tried to retire soon after the funeral, the Scotts still pay them to go out and maintain the place. They have put off making decisions about what to do with Marlo's things. Even her clothes are still in the house. Margaret offered to pack them up and give them to a charity, but Gloria told her to wait, she just wasn't ready to let anything go.

"Do you by any chance play the piano?" Tish asked, looking at Kat.

"Just a little, self-taught while I was hanging out with a friend who had a piano in her house. Why?"

"Marlo had a passion for music, she was really gifted and had a wonderful piano in the mansion." Tish explained. "I just wondered if you had that same gift." She paused. "Since you look exactly like her, I wondered if you might share the same talents."

"I would like to have taken lessons but I was reared by a single mother who kept us on a budget. It wasn't easy for her to manage on a secretary's salary so I didn't like to ask for extras."

There was a moment of silence before Tish interjected, "Well, Marlo had everything money could buy, but what she really wanted was what we all want, just to be happy, to be loved and useful." There was sadness in Tish's voice as she recalled her old friend.

"Kat, what are your immediate plans," Charles asked, "I imagine the Scotts will come here right away to meet you, I'll contact them today and get back to you. Where can I reach you?"

"I've been staying in the Radisson Hotel in Ashville," Kat said.

"That's a long way," Tish said, "why not stay here with me. I can fill you in on some things you might be interested in knowing, introduce you to the Hobsons. Oh, and, I'll introduce you to Zeger, Marlo's horse!"

"I love horses!" Kat exclaimed, "but I've only ridden once or twice with a friend from school."

"I wonder if Zeger will mistake you for Marlo. He has seemed a little down, not getting enough attention." Julie injected, "He's staying at my grandfather's stable. The Scotts gave him to Tish and me, told us to find him a good home. We haven't had the heart to let him go, so we just feed him and pet him. Pa sees that he is exercised though"

"If you're sure it's not any trouble," Kat said, "I will stay. I was thinking of changing hotels anyway, looking for something closer, perhaps in Knoxville or Maryville, so I went ahead and put all my stuff in the rental car. I'm kind of nervous about meeting my biological parents though."

"That's understandable," Charles said. "It's a very unusual situation, but they are fine people."

The young women left the office together with plans to get Kat settled in Tish's cottage before touring the Valley. Although Tish and Julie were very aware of the fact that Kat was not Marlo, their old feelings of comradery had returned.

"Remarkable," Julie murmured to herself.

Tish and Kat waved goodbye to Julie with plans to meet her later at Pa's Stables. Both Tish and Julie were eager to see how Zeger acted when he saw a human that looked like his old owner. They knew that horses remembered people and wondered if a horse recognized them merely by sight or by some other means.

They had seen twins before but never ones as identical as Kat and Marlo..

I'll bet Neil knows, Tish thought silently to herself as they drove to her cottage.

Kat was glad she was not going to have to search for a suitable hotel and surprised that she felt completely at ease in Tish's company. The cottage was warm and inviting, although somewhat cluttered and unorganized. She quickly became friends with Tyke, the little Terrier that leaped and barked a happy greeting as the pair entered.

"I'm sure you are tired from that long drive from Ashville, so please feel free to rest. You are not required to talk, you know," Tish said. Kat sat on the sofa and leaned back against it.

"I'm too excited, sad, and nervous to rest. I've had so much on my mind since my mother's letter . . . the woman I believed to be my mother . . . that I haven't really come to terms with her death. She was really the only family I knew all those growing up years. Now that I know that I have biological relatives, I'm happy about that, but I feel guilty for being happy. Does that make any sense?"

"Absolutely," Tish said, "you're being bombarded with so much emotional stuff all at once. Give yourself a break and don't worry about what you feel. Just acknowledge it and keep on living one day at a time. It will all sort itself out eventually."

"Thank you, Tish, for all of your kindness." Kat said, but I won't have a lot of time. If I don't get back to the *Globe* pretty soon, someone will take my place and I won't have a job to go back to. The paper never waits, there's always news."

"Oh, I forgot about your job. You said you are a reporter in Boston, didn't you?"

"Yes, with the *Boston Globe.* It's a newspaper there."

Tish was quiet, so deep in thought that Kat could almost imagine little wheels turning in her head.

"Why not look for a similar job here in the South, take time to get to know your kinfolks, your heritage, you know, all of it, everything that made you who you are."

"That is an idea, but newspaper jobs are not all that plentiful. I may not find one."

"Well, we need a newspaper here, that's for sure," Tish said.

"Tish, it costs a lot of money to put out a paper. You not only have to write the stories, you have to sell the advertising, make the ads, do formatting and graphics, distribution, and on and on. That's why newspapers have a staff, to cover so many jobs."

"Well, it's a thought." Tish was not going to say anything about the Scotts because she really didn't know how they would feel about Kat, but she believed they would happily finance a newspaper for her."

"There might be a way."

Tish left the room and came back with several scrapbooks and photograph albums which she unceremoniously plopped down on the coffee table.

"If you look through these, I'm sure you will recognize Marlo. You will feel like you are looking at yourself, I imagine."

Kat began turning the pages and caught her breath when she saw a photograph of Marlo for the first time.

"It's surreal," she said. "I suppose when one grows up with an identical twin, it would not be shocking. But, when I see her, it's so strange . . . like looking at myself wearing different clothes. No wonder Julie thought I was a ghost."

"Speaking of Julie," Tish said, glancing at her watch, she's probably already over at Pa's Stables waiting for us. Do you feel like going over and meeting the horse, Zeger?"

"Yes, I'm eager to meet him."

They drove to the stables, chatting non-stop as Tish pointed out places and answered questions as Kat tried to take in as much information as she could handle.

When Julie introduced Kat to her grandfather, he shook his head in amazement, "She told me you looked just like Marlo," he said, scratching his head and gesturing towards Julie, "but it's still rather shocking." After a slight pause, he continued, "Come on, let's go see what Zeger thinks."

They walked down the hallway in the barn toward his stall. To everyone's delight, Zeger raised his head, took one look at the people approaching his stall, then nickered and rushed to greet them. When Kat reached out to pet him, he began nuzzling her hand. When she came closer, he reached his head over the railing and put it on her shoulder with clear joy showing in his eyes.

"Well, would you look at that," Pa remarked, "I believe he thinks you're Marlo." Pa smiled as he watched

Zeger nuzzle Kat. "

"He's beautiful," Kat whispered, petting and staring at the animal.

"Whenever you want to ride him," Pa offered, "I'll tack him up and help you get adjusted to him. He'll probably be a little confused if you don't use the same cues Marlo used."

"I would like that," Kat said, "but I really don't know much about riding. I've only been on horses a few times, at places that rent horses, you know, where they put you on and the horse just follows the one in front of it."

"Well, we'll give you a crash course. You are surrounded with good teachers here. Both Julie and Tish have been riding all their lives and Zeger here is well trained." Pa gave Zeger a friendly slap and watched as Kat's expression became one of utter enchantment as she gazed at the horse.

"Okay! It's a deal, one day real soon." Kat put her arms around Zeger's neck and gave him a little soft hug, just the way Marlo used to do. Pa, Julie and Tish looked at each other, wondering how it was possible for two people to have the same gestures.

They left the stables and continued a sight-seeing drive through the countryside. Tish drove up the mountain and pointed out Crazy Creek and the small community that surrounded the bubbling fast water.

"I'm not sure what will happen to the creek if TVA goes ahead with their plans to back up the Little T and make a giant lake up here. It won't take the whole community, but it will definitely affect all of the creeks that run into the river downstream.

"But it is so beautiful here," Kat exclaimed. "And, with all of the man-made lakes around here, why on earth would they want another one?"

Tish spent the rest of the drive explaining the long struggle of the people against the Tellico Dam, and the gradual shift of public opinion due to the expert lobbying efforts of TVA, the media, and those who will profit from the taking of land from ordinary good citizens and giving it to the wealthy and well-connected.

"It's called capital-cronyism," Tish said. "And, we all recognize that it's probably too late to save the river, but we are still going to try. If we had had a good newspaper in the beginning of this thing, it might have helped educate the public, but the *Knoxville Journal* did publish many good letters and articles written by knowledgeable people, yet the powers that be went along with TVA."

When they returned to the cottage, Tish poured them a glass of Emmet Moss's wild fox grape wine. "It's pretty famous around here," Tish said, watching Kat nodding her satisfaction after tasting it for the first time.

"Last year, Dr. Etigener discovered the snail darter in the Little Tennessee River and thinks it is an endangered species. As you probably know, President Nixon created the Environmental Protection Agency (EPA), also last year. So, now, and I just found out about this, a lawyer who teaches at the University of Tennessee, Zygmunt Plater, and one of his students, Hank Hill, are going to file a lawsuit and try to stop the project because it will destroy the habitat of the darter. But first, I believe they have to get the little perch listed as an endangered species. I know it's a long shot, but I'm really glad the remaining landowners are going to try again to stop it. And, it's not just the landowners, it's also historians, sports enthusiasts, archeologists, and the Cherokee who don't want their ancient capitals and burial grounds destroyed. It's also people just like me who think it's just plain wrong to take a person's property and sell it to someone else. Of course, TVA and the University have already dug up lots of Cherokee bones and taken them for storage up there at UT somewhere."

"I'm confused about the names," Kat said, "why are they calling it the Tellico Dam when the Tellico River is up in Tellico Plains, and the dam is not on that river?"

"All the names around here make no sense at all," Tish said. "For example, the real Fort Loudoun, which will have to be moved or flooded, is close to Vonore, but the dam on the Big Tennessee River in Lenoir City was named Fort Loudoun, and the town of Loudon is not near the Fort either. Loudon is right on the Tennessee River but TVA put a sign up over one of the bridges that calls the river part of Watts Bar lake. The Watts Bar Dam is miles away down in Meigs County, I think. Anyway, it's not close. Poor little Loudon County has two TVA structures built in it, Fort Loudoun and the Tellico Dam. Only, the Tellico Dam isn't finished, the gates aren't ready to be closed and we hope they never will be. Yes, the names . . . utterly crazy, really."

"There sure is a lot to write about here." Kat exclaimed. "Sounds like every significant event in American history included some activity here, from the Cherokee villages to the fight with the British at the Fort before the Revolutionary War. It's amazing, really. No wonder there is so much devotion to this gorgeous land and the river. I hate it for you, this threat of seeing it all buried. I'm beginning to hate it for me too, and I just got here. Do you think it's in my biological roots?"

They smiled at each other.

"If you stay here, I'll introduce you to the hold-outs. The people who have refused to move. They are holding on, hoping for a miracle.

6
SCOTTS RETURN

Gloria and Ralph Scott were still in shock when they arrived at the airport and proceeded to the mansion where they would meet their biological daughter. Charles Jamison had assured them that the appearance of Katherine was not a hoax. They had been given the letter to read for themselves and had been in correspondence with the attorney in Boston who had represented the woman who had initially believed she was the mother of Kat instead of the deceased infant.

"It is so difficult to believe that all these years, we had no idea that we had another daughter," Gloria remarked when she was greeted by Charles Jamison and the Hobsons in front of the Scott mansion. "Is she here?"

"No, not yet. We thought you might be tired from the flight and want to rest before you met her. She's with Tish and I will phone her and tell her when she should come." He waited for an answer, seeing the doubt in their eyes as they looked at each other.

"If it's alright with you, Gloria, I'd like to meet her as soon as possible," Ralph said.

"Alright, I'll go in and telephone her now." They all entered the house. Their trusted long-time employees, the husband and wife Hobsons, had been there for hours, opening the place, removing sheets which had been covering the furniture. They had filled the refrigerator and put flowers in vases to make the rooms feel homey and inviting.

"Oh, Margaret," Gloria said, looking around, "you have certainly been busy because I remember how we left it."

Old Bill carried the luggage to the master bedroom. It was rather light because the Scott's had packed quickly, eager to meet their daughter.

Margaret served them coffee as they waited in the sitting room for Kat and Tish to arrive.

A short time later, the two young women walked in and Gloria swooned. Ralph also seemed stunned. Although they had been told that Kat was identical to Marlo, they could not help their reaction. Perhaps if Marlo were still alive, they would not have been overcome by the resemblance. After Gloria regained her composure, Charles made the introductions. In the background, they could hear Margaret saying, "Lordy, Lordy, it's Marlo's lost half!"

"I guess the letter said it all about why we never knew about you, but we are so very thankful to meet you now," Ralph explained. "We have so much to learn about each other. Would you be willing to leave Tish's cottage and come stay here with us so we can really get to know each other?"

Gloria reached out and gave Kat a hug, "Oh, it's just a miracle to have another daughter." She looked at the long, tawny blond curls, just like those Marlo had, and studied the face, absolutely identical. It was amazing!

Kat pondered the decision she had made about accepting their invitation to stay with them. Part of her wanted to remain with Tish where she felt comfortable, but she also wanted to know her biological parents while still grieving for the woman who reared her. What a jumble of feelings she would have to sort out. After several moments, she agreed to move into the Scott mansion.

"If it's alright with you," Kat said, I'll ride back with Tish to get my rental car and return with my clothes."

"That will be fine, dear." Gloria said, "Later, when you return, I'll show you Marlo's old room. You don't have to stay in it, we have plenty of other rooms, but I want you to see her clothes, in case you might want some of them. If you think they would make you uncomfortable wearing them, then, by all means, don't, but I have put off packing them away. She had all kinds of clothes including some beautiful outfits and I'm sure they would be a perfect fit."

"We will leave you all now, " Charles said. His task was over. He had carried out the arrangements for the Scotts to meet Marlo's twin, the baby they believed they had buried. There were still some legal issues to work through, for example the birth certificate, and the infant Martin's death certificate. Kat might wish to change her name. All that could wait. These strangers must have time to know each other.

After Tish and Kat followed Charles out, Margaret asked Gloria if she thought it would be appropriate to prepare a meal with some of Marlo's favorite foods. "I don't know if twins like the same thing or not, do you?"

"No," Margaret, I have no idea, but it seems more likely than not. Let's see for ourselves. But, you're such a good cook, anyone would probably like whatever you decide to fix."

Bill was outside, humming as he worked. October was a busy time for gardeners, preparing planting beds for the cool weather annuals, especially pansies, and taking care of shrubs and blooming autumn flowers, especially the chrysanthemums. There was plenty of mulching to do. Although he knew there was uncertainty about the future of the Scott Mansion, he was determined to keep the grounds in good shape as long as he was able. And, he believed that the new daughter in there would mean a rebirth of the place. He and Margaret had worked there for so long, it felt like a second home to them. Sure, they could stay home in their rocking chairs, but they had great pride in the Scott place and wanted to see it maintained, even if they moved slower than they used to. Everyone knew they were responsible for how it looked and they enjoyed the compliments they had received through the years.

Margaret took a glass of freshly made iced tea out to Bill and carried a glass for herself. It was time for them to take a break; they sat on a garden bench below a giant White Oak that shaded them from the sun. While they were resting and enjoying the sweet tea, Margaret happened to glance at the driveway and noticed that Charles was walking to his car. She jumped up and approached him as fast as her wobbly old legs could move.

"Mr. Jamison," she called, "when are they ever going to have the trial for that murderer? It's been a year and they still haven't had it. I just don't understand. I want it over with. It's going to be hard on them," she motioned towards the house with her head.

"I know, Margaret. I wish there was a way we could make it happen faster. If Alex Morgan would only plead guilty, it would be easier on everyone, even him. But he and his lawyer are determined to drag it out as long as they can." He shook his head.

"At least they have him locked up with no chance of bail. He did plead guilty to the assaulting Tish, because he was caught in the act, and is serving time for that charge. In addition to that, he has been charged with the attempted murder of Tish as well as the murder of Marlo. So, I feel certain he is going to remain behind bars. Still, it would be best for all to get the trial over with. "

Margaret sighed, "I understand you can't do anything about it, but I just keep hoping. I dread having to go into court and reliving that terrible day we found Marlo."

As Charles drove away, he wondered if Alex knew about Marlo's newly discovered twin. Perhaps not. The Scotts had not made any public announcement about Kat. Wonder what would happen if old Alex saw her for the first time in the courtroom. That would be something to witness. He had no sympathy whatever for the man who had beaten Tish nearly to death, but he did feel sorry for Mary, the man's innocent wife who had moved out of state with their children and was trying to start a new life.

She, too, had begged Alex to plead guilty for the sake of their children so that they could move on without having to think about a trial. Alex, however, was determined to say he was not guilty of killing Marlo although he had admitted it to Tish before he assaulted her.

Back in Tish's cottage, while Kat was packing, she confided in Tish that she felt a little strange going to stay with the people who were still strangers to her.

"I can imagine," Tish said, "just remember, I'm still here and available to rescue you if it gets to be too much to take in. It's a different world for you, I suppose.

"I know we've just known each other for a couple of days, but I feel like I've known you all my life. I hope it doesn't upset you by my saying this, but it's almost like you are Marlo."

"You know, it's strange, but I feel like a whole person now. It's kind of like half of me was somewhere else but now I'm all here. Do you think it's possible that Marlo's spirit has joined me?"

"I don't know, Kat. I've never known an identical twin before. I don't know what it must be like. I've heard stories that one twin can feel the pain the other experiences."

"Well, I don't know about that, but I have had a few aches and pains for no apparent reason. Perhaps they were some of Marlo's hurts of some kind. And, one day last year around this time, I became very sad. I had worked late one night writing an article after a long meeting and the next day, I took a rare nap in the afternoon. Anyway, I was having a nightmare about someone choking me; when I woke up, I became incredibly depressed. The sadness stayed with me for several days before I could shake it off and get on with my day-to-day life. Now, I can't help but wonder if that was when Marlo was being choked."

"Can you go back and find out what day that was? It might be interesting to find out if it was the same day Marlo was murdered."

"I suppose I could look at the newspaper's archives and see when the meeting was held." They continued in silence wondering about a possible connection between Kat and Marlo's spirit. Then Tish remembered the old lady who lived up beyond Crazy Creek.

"One of these days," she said, "I'll take you up on the mountain to meet Gertrude. She's what we call a 'seer' in these parts. She's supposed to have the gift of seeing into the spirit world. I get chills sometimes, just listening to some of the things she says. I don't know whether to believe her or not, but she is a good woman and helps a lot of people. And, you know the Bible says we should judge by the fruits . . . or something like that."

Kat smiled, "One of these days, but not now. I can't even get my head wrapped around all that's going on."

It didn't take Kat long to collect her things and put them in the rental car. She promised Tish that she would phone soon and arrange to go trail riding with her and Julie, after a few more sessions in the round pen with Zeger.

"You'll love seeing the places Zeger can take you! You'll have a whole different perspective from the back of a horse."

Kat felt rather odd driving back to the Scott mansion. The estate was impressive and rather daunting to someone like herself who was from the lower-middle income bracket while the Scotts were obviously in the upper bracket.

When she arrived, Gloria met her at the door and eagerly gave her a tour of the house. "You can choose any one of these bedrooms," Gloria explained, "but I do want to show you Marlo's old room in case you would prefer it."

They walked further down the hallway on the second floor until they came to an open door that led into a large room. It had a pleasant ambiance with sun filtering in through the eyelet ruffles of the curtains. The room was cool from fresh mountain air because someone had opened the windows to freshen the place after it had been shut tight for so long.

"Margaret just closed the windows a short time ago so it hasn't had time to warm up."

"It feels good," Kat said, "not cold, just refreshing."

Gloria opened a door that led into a room-size closet filled with clothing, still hanging in the same place as it was before Marlo's death."

"Like I said before, these were Marlo's clothes. I know I should have done something with them before, but I just couldn't. Now, I'm hoping there was a reason why I kept them. Do you think you could go through them and see if you would like to keep anything? Then, Margaret and I will pack up the rest and give them to charity, before they all go out of style."

"I thought I would feel bad being in her room," she told Gloria, "but I don't. I even feel like I belong in here as opposed to the other rooms. Do you mind if I choose her room? It would make it easier for me to go through the clothes." Kat was surprised at how natural she felt to be in Marlo's room.

"No, dear," Gloria said, "it pleases me. This room was so sad without her. Now, it feels kind of like dear Margaret said, that Marlo's other half is home."

After Gloria left, Kat sat down on the bed and looked around her, trying to take in the myriad of feelings the room evoked in her. There was so much to do, both here and there. She was going to have to leave and go back to Boston. If she wanted to keep her job with the *Globe*, she was going to have to get back there soon. Her employers had been patient, but it was time to make a decision about when that would be. She had better tell the Scotts before they made plans. It was not something she should put off.

Kat went back downstairs and found Ralph and Gloria in the cozy little alcove they spent most of their time in.

"I appreciate so much how welcome you have made me feel and I must say, I love it here, but . . ." she sighed, "I've got so much unfinished business to do in Boston. I have to take care of Mother's estate, you know, close out her affairs, and also, get back to my job or I will lose it. But, I hope you will invite me back." Kat didn't notice Gloria wince when she spoke of the woman who reared her as her mother.

"Oh, but we have just found you! We can't let go of you so soon." Gloria fought back tears.

"I'm sorry that I have upset you," Kat said.

"Listen, Kat," Ralph interjected. "Why don't you just quit that job of yours and come here. We'll find you something to do. In fact, we've been trying to get someone to start a newspaper here. If we'd had a good, honest, truth-telling publication in the past, some of the heartache of displaced persons might have been avoided. We aren't sure of that, but it might have helped stop the brain-washing going on by the TVA crowd."

"Tish said the same thing," Kat recalled. "A newspaper does seem to have influence, sometimes."

"What do you say, then?" Ralph asked. "We have no close kin but you, and we have more money than we need, so how about it? Will you let us finance a newspaper here in the area. Or, you can always apply to work for one of the papers already in existence. Whatever you want to do. We just want to make up for lost time with our daughter."

"Are you sure? I do feel like I belong here, like I

have always been Southern. Do you think it's in the genes?"

Ralph and Gloria both laughed, relieved that they were not going to lose this daughter right away.

"I think I'll apply for a job with one of the other newspapers, at least until I get the lay of the land, so to speak. Then, we'll go from there. I may not get hired, you know." Kat said. "But, first, I've got to tie up loose ends."

Kat was flooded with a sense of relief. A decision had been made. She believed it was the right one.

"We do understand that you have things to take care of back in Boston and if we can help in any way, just let us know. We'll be right here when you return, but we also have things to take care of back in Florida. We left rather abruptly when we learned of your existence."

* * *

Kat decided she should go on back to Boston now while it was still autumn and close out her former life there. She was looking forward to starting a new life in Tennessee so she abruptly booked a flight out of the Maryville/Knoxville airport for the next day. Since she still had the rental car, there was no need for anyone to take her, but someone would have to pick her up when she returned.

"I purchased a round-trip ticket so I can return in two weeks," she smiled, "is that all right?"

"Definitely!" the Scotts rose and hugged her. She hugged them back. They did feel a strong bonding kinship with each other and were warmed by the realization of having a family.

"I think I'll phone Tish now and tell her what I've decided, if that's okay."

"You are our grown daughter, dear, you don't need our approval for what you do here. I know it must be strange, but try to feel like this is your home, not just ours. In fact, we have spent more time living in Florida than here for years. It was always more Marlo's home than ours. She was determined to stay here and keep her grandfather's legacy alive."

Kat smiled and excused herself to make the phone call. Tish answered right away and was happy to hear that Kat was going to come back permanently.

"Since you're leaving tomorrow, I imagine you've got packing to do, but I'll see you when you get back. I'm very glad about the way things are working out." Tish said.

After hanging up the phone, Tish grabbed her jacket and left. She was eager to see Neil who was growing impatient with her for being so preoccupied with Kat, although he did understand why.

She jumped into the truck and drove to Neil's place. She saw him astride a two-year old gelding that he was in the process of training. When he saw her, he dismounted and walked to the rail of the round pen to meet her.

"It's about time," he said as he circled her in his arms and smiled. "I can't afford to hire help so I've got to hold onto you," he said teasingly.

She pushed him away in playful rebuke, and then said, "I've missed you. Seems like it's been forever since we've spent any time together. But, guess what, Kat's coming back to stay."

"So, I'm going to have to deal with another threesome, you, Julie, and Kat." Neil shook his head.

"When she gets back and settled in, I'm going to take her around and introduce her to the dam-resistors, you know, the folks that are holding out until the bitter end. Although she didn't grow up here, she really appreciates the river and the land."

7
EXPLORING ON HORSEBACK

During the two weeks that Kat was gone, Tish and Julie went trail-riding as often as they could, taking advantage of the perfect October weather. Often, Neil would go too, and sometimes even Pa Ferguson, especially when he wanted to find out if a trade horse was dependable. He had a reputation to uphold. He was known for telling the truth to prospective buyers of his horses. They spent many hours riding in and around Citico and wondered how much the proposed lake would affect the area.

"I love it here," Julie said as they rested their horses in the shallows of the creek, letting the horses drink.

"Me, too," Tish echoed. "Did you know that TVA already has 2500 linear miles of impounded former-rivers between 60-plus dams? Tennessee has more slack-water shoreline than all the Great Lakes combined!"

"No, I didn't know that."

"I'm quoting from Zyg Plater. You know, the law professor that's helping Hank Hill file a lawsuit using the newly discovered snail darter."

"Do you think they have a chance of stopping it?" Julie asked.

"Well, a lot happened last year. It was in August when Dr. David Etneir discovered the endangered snail darter at Coytee Springs in the shoals on the Little T. And, then, in December, President Nixon signed the Endangered Species Act which says that federal agencies can't harm endangered species or habitats. So, if the legal eagles can walk through the hoops before them, they do have a chance. First, though, they have to get the snail darter on the list of Endangered Species and, also, get the Little T named as its critical habitat. They'll have to go to Washington and petition the Department of Interior to put the darter on the list. There might be pitfalls there, I really don't know."

They also rode in the valley around Fort Loudoun and watched some of the excavation going on. Archeologists had been busy trying to discover and preserve what artifacts they could find where so much history was evident beneath layers of rich top soil.

Neil was interested in the Fort and remembered learning some things about it in history classes during his youth.

"It was the first Anglo settlement west of the Alleghenies, completed in 1757," Tish reminded him. "It was surrendered to the Cherokees in August of 1760. If it weren't for Alice Milton who is on some history board, TVA would have already destroyed it. She has really had to fight to save it. TVA planned to flood it and put it under their lake, but Mrs. Milton made so much noise about it, trying to stop the dam as well as save the Fort, TVA decided to move it, build up the ground where it was, and then put it back; in other words, raise it 17 ft from its original setting."

Neil shook his head. There were no words that came to mind to explain the stretch of TVA.

The valley housed a vibrant farming community where excessive yields of corn, soybeans, pasture, hay and a variety of other crops were produced. Goldkist had a grain elevator in Greenback where farmers could sell what they produced. Combines and tractors and wagons were sold at the numerous farm dealerships in the area. Dairying was also big business on some farms, as well as a tree nursery on Rose Island. But, much of the activity was disappearing now, as many people did what was pragmatic, giving up and moving out. It had happened to some of them before, when previously owned farms on other rivers were taken for other dams. Some valley resident families had been condemned from land in earlier years, from around Norris, Watts Bar, Fontana, Douglas, or from any one of the many other area dams previously built by TVA. Several of these families just wanted to get the move over with. There was just no way to win when their own government sold you out, they knew.

"Imagine, being run off your land not once but twice," Julie said. "Imagine needing to build a new fence to keep your livestock penned while wondering if it would be bulldozed away. As much as I wish the farmers would stay and hold on, I can see why they feel the need to find land somewhere else, someplace that isn't threatened yet, anyway." Julie said.

"When Kat gets back and starts working down here as a reporter, you're going to have to help me catch her up on the history of this horrific project. Most people have no idea what all we've been through," Tish remarked.

"Oh, I will, definitely. It makes me mad when I hear them referring to the farms as *undeveloped*; they don't think about all the buildings, the labor that's gone into the fields. You know, it takes years to eliminate old sage grass if the soil hasn't been limed to the correct PH level. Some farmers have spent years moving rocks and old stumps to create permanent pastures that look more like golf courses."

The following day, Pa and Neil said they had too much work to do at their home stables to go trail riding, but Julie and Tish decided to go again because the weather was so perfect.

"This is really a special day for riding . . . not too cold, but cool enough; no flies and bees will threaten us, and not too hot or windy or wet." Tish said.

"I know," Julie said, "only I'm a little sore from yesterday; must be out-of-shape. We did ride a long time."

"Let's stop by and see the Ritchey farm on our way back. They'll know the latest about the river." Tish suggested. "

They meandered along the river, stopping to enjoy views of places they had long treasured. Other riders were also taking advantage of the day, enjoying the trails. They ran into a couple of friends they often rode with, Marsha Standridge and Chris Carpenter. After exchanging pleasantries, they waved and moved on slowly enjoying cool gentle breezes, pausing to rest the horses in one special place, then another.

"I'm ready to go now. I think Nutmeg is just plain tuckered out." Julie said smiling, remembering how Neil had laughed when he had learned that both of their horses were named after spices; Tish's mare was named Ginger and hers, Nutmeg. He said he thought he'd give some of his new horses the rest of the spice rack names, starting with cloves, cinnamon and sage.

They rode back to the horse trailer and drove to the Ritchey farm where they pulled onto the shoulder of the road by the entrance to the property. Mary Ann Ritchey was sweeping the front porch of the lovely two story farmhouse. It was lined with white rocking chairs positioned comfortably behind a myriad of hanging plants.

"Hi," she said brightly. "Where have you all been with your horses?"

"We've been riding in the valley up around the Fort, what's left of it, and talking about the new efforts to save the river. How's it going?"

"We're hopeful." Mary Ann said. "Some of us are going to Washington pretty soon. Zyg and Hank, along with Dr. Eitenger, are going to try to get the darter on the list of Endangered Species. You know, Beryl Moser has already been up there at least ten times, maybe more."

"How many landowners are holding out, refusing to take the money TVA is offering?"

"There aren't too many of us left. You know, after they built the dam structure, most just gave up, but Asa McCall and his wife Nellie are not going to give up and neither are we. And, of course, Beryl, is definitely going to stay on. We did find out that this land where we are standing, where the house is, will not be under water but they seem determined to take it anyway. As you know, 16,000 acres of land is going to be flooded but they are taking 40,000 acres. How is that possible here in the United States!"

"It is hard to believe. If only the national news had gotten the whole story out early on, it might have made a difference. But, they don't seem interested in covering anything going on down here in the South unless it's something they can make fun of. Seems like they love to show some bad act being done by some lame-brain, as if we are all the same."

"But some of our locals are lame-brains or they wouldn't go along with whatever TVA wants." Julie interjected.

Mary Ann nodded, then said, "I don't know why some people don't appreciate the farm economy. You know, the export of farm products right now is about the only thing keeping the country from having a terrible trade deficit. And, just think about the money being made by the people manufacturing all the tractors, combines, and everything else needed for all these crops we sell. Some in government think only certain areas of the nation should farm. They want to force industrialization on us here. I just don't know why. It's much better to have crops growing all over the country because bad weather events can wipe out crops. If there's a drought out west, it may be good weather here and vice versa." She paused, shook her head and gazed at the river moving through the fields.

"I remember when the Tennessee Farm Bureau Federation adopted an anti-Tellico Resolution, back in '64 when TVA was getting their promotion rolling." Mary Ann said, " It was reported by the University of Tennessee and others that $4-million per year of farm income would be lost with the taking of 39,000 acres of prime land, plus the loss of the ripple effect from supply businesses, processors, retailers and others."

"You do know you're preaching to your own choir, don't you?" Julie said.

Smiling, Mary Ann replied. "Oh, I know you two agree with me, but sometimes I just have to vent. We've lived with anxiety for so long now, hoping and dreading, both at the same time, knowing the odds of anyone beating TVA are not good. And farming is how our family makes its living. Sally and I are going to be teachers but, you know, my brother and our parents depend on the farm for their total income. And, our sister Carolyn is still a kid in school."

The young women stood silent for a minute, shaking their heads.

Finally Tish said, "I hate it for you. And, I hate it for all of us, for the people, the country, everyone, because our founding fathers never intended for the law of eminent domain to be used as a tool for capital cronyism. Congress should never have let TVA become so powerful."

"I heard that the Davis family finally found a lawyer to represent them against TVA in the condemnation of their farm and what they want to pay. Their farm, over 200 acres, was settled by their family in 1863. They've got a cemetery there where family members are buried. TVA has offered them only $43,000 for their farm, house, and barns. They have filed a suit, but they can't get a jury trial. It's a shame that these condemnation cases go before a Federal Judge who naturally sides with the Federal agency and their appointed appraisers. It's different when the State condemns land for roads. If you get a good lawyer to represent you, you usually do well in front of a jury of your peers."

Suddenly, the sound of a horse pawing in the trailer caused Tish to realize how much time had passed.

"We got to get these horses home; been gone too long now. Our folks will be worried. See you, Mary Ann."

They climbed back in the truck, waved and left.

8
KAT COMES HOME

Although she was leaving Boston where she had lived most of her life, Kat felt like she was going home. Perhaps there was an undefinable link with her genetic past because she felt like she belonged with the Scotts. In spite of the love she felt for the woman who had mistakenly taken her as a baby from the hospital in Ashville, she had decided to have her surname restored to what it would have rightfully been. She was going to keep her given name. She couldn't imagine being called anything besides Katherine or Kat. The name change was something the Scotts had discussed with her before she left for Boston. She knew they would be pleased with her decision.

One of the first things she was going to have to do was purchase an automobile. One couldn't very well become a reporter here without means of transportation. She hadn't needed or wanted a car in Boston because it was easier to take a cab or bus or walk in the city to cover the beat she was assigned. She chose to purchase a spunky-looking little Jeep at the advice of Julie and Tish who seemed to know where she would need to go. Then, they rode with her around the entire area, pointing out landmarks, people and significant information.

"I'll never be able to remember all of this. Slow down and educate me a little at a time," she pleaded.

They were eager for her to meet the landowners who were still defying TVA's efforts to buy them out. They took her first to meet Beryl Moser. He was a mailman who lived in his family home in Vonore.

After introductions were made, he invited them to sit down. The middle-aged bachelor stood straight with the erect military posture he had maintained. Still living an active lifestyle, hunting with his dogs, and fishing the Little T, he appeared more youthful than his years and exhibited a passion for the area in his speech. There was nothing insincere about the man, Kat thought, and it was clear that he loved his home.

"Tell me about yourself," Kat said. "Remember, I'm new here so I know nothing about you, just that you want to keep your place."

"Well," Beryl said, gesturing to the solid well-built home where they were sitting, "I don't own as much as the others who own large farms. This is it, this house and the out buildings and the five acres it sits on. But, it's home and I want to stay here. My father built this house back in the '20's. My parents had three children, me and two sisters. I was 12 years old when my father died so I had to grow up pretty quick and help my mother as much as I could." He sighed and took a deep breath before continuing.

"When I was eighteen years old, I was drafted into the army to go fight in Korea. I listed my mother as a dependent so she could get my pay because she needed whatever little bit of money she could get. There was some mix-up and she didn't receive any money. But, finally, someone got in touch with Senator Estes Kefauver who was from our county over in Madisonville, and he got it straightened out. At that time, I was a Democrat, like Kefauver. But after all this TVA business, I am no longer anything; I vote for the person, not the party, because people in both political parties are guilty. They have not protected the interests of the people who live here, although some from both parties have tried, at least for a while. Then, TVA gets to them one way or another. They threaten to have them defeated if they oppose the project, and they are very successful in doing that by supporting their opponents, with paid advertisements, billboards, newspaper endorsements, all that kind of thing." Beryl paused, then continued .

Later, as Kat reviewed the political history in the area and the state, she saw what Beryl meant. TVA was able to support and elect Democrats to the positions of County Judge in Loudon County after their attempt at blackmailing former Judge Ben B. Simpson. Prior to the election, TVA representatives visited his home and told him in no uncertain terms, they would find a candidate to oppose him and defeat him if he continued to oppose the project. Judge Simpson, of course, continued to stand with the opponents. The local newspaper endorsed his opponent, who also headed a local development board. In the end, although Simpson was defeated, he carried every precinct in Loudon County except two Democrat strongholds. In Lenoir City where totals were numerically questionable, the votes nevertheless gave TVA another mouthpiece.

Still, the opposition rallied and the fight continued. In the next election, TVA's candidate was defeated for reelection, by a Republican who was an opponent of the TVA project. However, much damage had been done to their cause during the TVA proponent's tenure. After a long succession of Democrat governors elected by citizens of Tennessee, a Republican, Dr. Winfield Dunn, was elected in 1971. And , a Republican Bill Brock was elected to the U.S. Senate that same year. Both were opposed to the Tellico Project and had voiced their objections during their campaigns. So, the pendulum kept swinging as the people of Tennessee kept trying to find leaders to truly represent them. But, funding had already been given in 1965 when President Johnson put the Tellico Dam in his budget. Later, when representatives sought to move the funds to other projects with less opposition, TVA dug their heels in and put what some members of the Knoxville Chamber of Commerce called "unseemly pressure" on organizations and individuals to pressure Congress for the project. TVA flew people by the droves to D.C., and allegedly told them where to go and suggested what they say, meanwhile threatening opponents in various ways, primarily with the vote.

One of the men who TVA took to D.C. was Knoxville attorney Ray Jenkins who had owned a farm within the taking line established by TVA. At first, he was reported to be against the project but after being offered $173,650 for his farm, he was for it. And, Dr. Troy Bagwell who was paid $496,616 for his farm accepted TVA's offer very early in the buying process. These men did not farm for a living nor did they have an attachment to the land they owned. They were paid more than other landowners were offered, theoretically, because they could influence others to go ahead and sell.

Kat was quickly absorbing how and why there were shifting loyalties with the Tennessee voters, yet TVA was so powerful, they continued to get their way, in spite of the independent opinion of the majority.

Beryl continued to explain, "For example, Tish's father, a Republican, tried to stop it and so did Senator Bill Brock, a Republican. When I go to Washington to talk to people, to try to get them to help us save the river and the land, Senator Brock has always been very helpful to me. He'd send someone to meet me at the airport. He tries his best but you just wait and see, he'll cave or get beat in his next election. That's what happens to all of the ones who go against TVA. All those government employees seem to stick together. They're all on the public dole. TVA has the money and means to get their way. And, they're not just after the river, they're after the land.

"You see, this spot here won't be flooded but they want to take it anyway. Why? To make money on, that's the only reason. It's going to be lakefront property. The lake is going to cover 16,000 acres but they are trying to take 40,000 acres! They say it's for industry, jobs. We all know that's hogwash because the land-owners have offered to sell tracts of land to industry if they can just keep the rest of their farms, but TVA says "No." The harder we fight, the more determined they seem to be to kill the river, especially Hall, that mayor up in Tellico Plains. "

Kat shook her head. "I've covered a lot of crime and bad stuff for the *Globe* up in Boston, but nothing like this. I really had no idea our government could con-demn and take land for no good reason. I thought emi-nent domain was only done for roads that had to go through properties in order to connect. I can under-stand why they couldn't zig-zag major roads around every parcel that someone didn't want to sell, but this is ridiculous."

"So you understand how we feel?" Tish asked.

"Of course. Mr. Moser, how much money have they offered you?"

"Call me Beryl," he said. "At first, they said they'd give me $200 an acre. That's what they've conned some folks into taking. They try to get it as cheap as they can. And that's for the buildings and all. The average of what they're paying folks is $380 an acre no matter what's on it. The only reason the average is that high is because of the people who had mortgages on their farms, you know, amounts that were loaned based on previous appraisals by the lending institutions. TVA had to pay more to those folks to satisfy the lenders."

Kat shook her head again, murmuring almost to

herself, "And you are a veteran. Imagine that, going to Korea to fight for the country and then coming home and having to face this kind of fight." She sighed remembering the photo of the soldier she had believed to be her father and his death on a battlefield so many years ago.

"I spent three years and one month in the U.S. Army . . ." Beryl said, looking into space, seeing the past. "I served on the 38th parallel in Korea when I got there and was still there when I left. We had much better weapons in training here in the states than we had over there. The weapons we had to use in the real fight were leftovers from World War II." He chuckled at the absurdity.

"At 22 years old, I achieved the rank of E-5 and I was told I was the youngest to ever achieve that rank." Instead of boasting about it, Beryl smiled and said, "I don't know if Senator Kefauver had anything to do with it or not." It was as if it was difficult for him to accept the fact that he probably earned the rank.

"I'm sure you were an outstanding soldier," Kat said, "Tennesseans have a reputation, you know, don't forget all the heroes that have come out of this state, going back to Davy Crockett, and before we were even a state. And, in more recent history, don't forget about that famous soldier from over in Fentress County. What was his name?

"You talking about Alvin York?" Beryl asked.

"Oh, yes," that was his name. Gary Cooper played him in a movie." Kat said.

"You sure know a lot of Tennessee history to be

from somewhere else, " Beryl commented.

"But I was born in Ashville and my mother bragged a great deal about both North Carolina and Tennessee, so I really feel like I'm from that mountain range, which ever state it happens to be in." Kat gestured to the horizon of smoky blue mountains.

Beryl reached down and scratched behind the ears of the hound that sat by his chair looking balefully up at his master, waging his tail and seeming to enjoy the pleasant autumn day.

Kat and Tish said their goodbyes and began the drive home.

Silent for a while, Kat said, "I just can't get over the fact that Beryl is a veteran . . . it doesn't seem fair."

"Nothing about this is fair," Tish said. "And Beryl isn't the only Korean veteran who has suffered. Don Steele lost a leg in Korea and suffered four injuries in six months. In addition to his four purple hearts he won two bronze stars for bravery. The Steele family owned land on the Little T so after Don returned to Monroe County, he married, built a house, a store for boaters, two barns and two wells on Highway 72. They were located on the north side of the river.*

"Ancestors of the Steele family came into the area way back in the seventeen hundreds. They first settled up around Cades Cove until eminent domain took that home and land for the Great Smoky Mountain National Park. The family then walked to their next home, which would later be taken for the Fontana Dam. So, that was twice the Steeles were forced to move. Now this project is taking another one of their places, business and home.

"Joey Steele, one of Don's sons recalls fishing the shoals of the Little T from the back of a mule called Jack. He loved life on and near the river. It was a grand place to grow up in. The Indian mounds and Chota were on the South side of the river so the Steeles named their boat dock 'Chota' and put up a sign that read, 'Have boat, will float.' His brother had cabins called the River Breeze which he rented out, mainly to fisherman. Don Steele would guide them on fishing trips. It was a good business for Don to be in, something he could easily do with his one good leg. They sold bait, cold drinks, gas, and rented boats. Their kids learned business from their parents. Those kids even knew how much the electric bill was along with everything else. They worked together as a family, putting the boats in the river and taking them out from various places after they floated downstream. Although they certainly weren't getting rich, they seemed to be living a wonderful life."*

Kat sat spellbound as Tish recalled and shared more of local history, "In the sixties, Don Steele got the letter from TVA telling him they wanted to buy the land. He declined and held onto the land, but about nine years later, he suffered a massive heart attack and died. His wife felt she had no choice but to accept TVA's offer. In 1973, TVA paid her $23,000 for the business, two wells, boat house, store, two barns and a five bedroom house. Imagine that small amount of money for all of that!

*From interview by Frances Dorward in *Damgreed*.

Mrs. Steele moved her family to a run-down place on Highway 129, and had to go into debt to pay for it, even though it wasn't anything as nice as what they had before.

"Then, she got a second blow. Her husband's pension for his army service was stopped. She, along with other widows of the war has met with various committees trying to get the pension reinstated to help her raise her children. I hope they can. They're really struggling, living mainly on fish the boys catch. Where they are now, I don't think they have much of a place for a big garden like they used to have, but I'm not sure. I haven't been over there."

There was sadness and anger in her voice as Tish explained the situation.

Kat shook her head. "That is terrible! I thought the law of eminent domain stated that property owners were to be compensated in kind so they could replace what was taken."

"If you read the law, it pretty much does say that but these TVA appraisers just plain lie. I don't know how else to say it. They should have to go out and find similar property and pay the price." Tish said.

"I wish I had been here sooner writing about all of this." Kat said, "Now, with so many people gone, already moved out and everyone making fun of the snail darter, I'm probably trying to tilt a windmill."

9

CHRISTMAS SEASON

Neil trudged through the mud and ice to the barns to feed and water the horses before having his own breakfast. He could feel the cold even through his heavy Carhardt coat and decided it was time to get out his insulated coveralls. The horses were neighing and snorting, glad to hear the familiar sound of his footsteps walking toward them. They knew their feed would soon be placed in their troughs. He loaded his shiny, new wheelbarrow with grain and a scoop and pushed it down the hallway from one stall to the next, giving each horse it's particular ration. After the grain was fed, he repeated his route hoisting flakes of green timothy and orchard grass hay into each manger. Last came the water buckets. Neil dragged the long hose up and down the hallway, filling each bucket with water. One of these days, he might install automatic waterers. But, first, there would have to be more income, much more, he mused.

Back in his warm kitchen, Neil put some bacon in a frying pan and got eggs and butter out of the refrigerator. As he cooked his breakfast, his thoughts went to Tish. He missed her. Ever since Kat had come to the valley, he had seen less and less of Tish. Although he definitely understood their passion for the river and appreciated all they were trying to do, he missed having Tish around. After her near death experience when Alex Morgan almost killed her, he had seen her almost every day during the long weeks that followed as she slowly healed from the vicious attack. After she was released from the hospital, she stayed for a while at her parents' home but had visited him nearly every day, keeping him company while he worked, assisting him when she could. Neil knew he needed to hire some part-time help but had delayed because of finances and also, he realized, because he just didn't trust strangers with his horses. He had met lots of people since buying the farm but not many job-seekers. Maybe he'd ask Tish or her father if they knew anyone he could hire. But, that would be after Christmas. He wouldn't be able to travel to Middle Tennessee to spend Christmas with his parents. Maybe they could come here. He decided he'd give them a call and ask them, although the house didn't have much furniture. There was a bed in one of the two extra bedrooms with nothing else in it, not even a chair. But, that'd be acceptable for his parents. But, they probably wouldn't want to leave his siblings.

Neil ate his breakfast, still pondering what he should do about Christmas gifts. He'd been too busy to shop. He figured he could pick up something quickly at the Farmers Coop for his father and maybe find something for his mother at the Pharmacy; it offered quite a variety of gift items, like books, boxed chocolates, perfumed lotions, that sort of thing. But Tish . . what he really wanted to give her was a ring. He never had come right out and asked her to marry him, but she surely knew. He had told her how much he loved her. Surely, she knew he wanted to marry her. It was just that money had been so limited, he felt he should wait until he was more secure. But, if he didn't go ahead and get her a ring, what else could he give her that wouldn't be trivial. Shoot, he decided, I'm going to go ahead and buy her a ring. I'll find out what size she wears from Julie. I think I can trust her to keep a secret.

That decided, Neil rubbed his face and decided it was time to shave. He glanced in the mirror and saw a happy man with a twinkle in his clear, smiling eyes, and a tuff of sun-bleached hair protruding from the toboggan on his head. He laughed at his reflection and said to the Border Collie at his heels, "If she could see me now, she'd probably say 'No'."

Meanwhile, Rebecca Jamison was busy preparing for Christmas. She realized that, as the years passed swiftly by, it was getting more difficult to prepare for the crowd that would be flocking home for the holidays. Although she loved her children, they seemed to take her for granted, not realizing that the years had taken a toll and made her weary of all the cooking and decorating. She hardly recognized the aging face she encountered in every mirror that she passed nor did the salt and strangely red streaks in her once auburn hair seem familiar without the shine it once had. And, there were more and more little lines appearing here and there around her mouth and eyes. Growing old was accompanied with more problems than she ever imagined when she was younger. But, thankful that she could still do most of the things she had always done, she plodded on.

Charles had finally agreed to buy an artificial tree, although he much preferred to go cut a real one. She wanted an artificial one so she could put it up early and get that task out of the way. Tish had done most of the decorating for her this year, making wreaths and sprays for the doors and stringing lights on the box-woods in the yard. And the freezer was full of made-ahead rolls and biscuits and cornbread for stuffing, Today she was making cakes to also freeze, trying to get ahead so she would have time later for all those dishes that had to be made at the last minute. Wonder why people always seemed to prefer the dishes that required the most work? Why did growing old make some traditions so tiresome? She missed the spirit that used to come with the season and told herself she would do whatever it took to shed her darkened mood. But, nothing she could do would bring back the friends she missed, all those good people who had moved away, forced out by the TVA's condemnation of their property for their damn dam!

The Christmas season was a major time of year for all Christian churches, but services in a number of those in the area were somber reminders of what was lost as sanctuaries were not near as full because of the families who had been forced to move. The vacant places in the pews reminded the Jamison family of the Graham family among others who were now gone. That family had moved to Loudon many years ago having been forced out by an earlier TVA dam on the Big T. Bill Graham and his son Jim were successful and highly respected farmers who owned a farm on the Little T. Jim was a young man, married with young children. He didn't want to leave but he knew, as his family had learned before, that TVA had ungodly power. He could not risk buying seed to sow in fields that might be taken from him before he could harvest what was planted. He didn't have the heart to build new fences or make sorely needed additions to the milking parlor knowing they would soon be bulldozed into a heap. So he had taken the money that was offered and with a heavy heart set out to buy him a different farm. He had only 18 months to reinvest the money and avoid paying a capital gains tax. It's difficult to find a good farm that one can afford to buy. He finally found what he was looking for up along the French Broad River. Neil had helped the family move their livestock. It was quite a task to move all the farm equipment, cattle, horses, household goods, stored hay, everything that was needed to operate a farm. The Graham children were missed by their friends in school, and the familiar empty pews in the Cumberland Presbyterian Church where his family had worshipped were also reminders of their absence.

As Rebecca sat in church, she could not help but feel deep resentment that bordered on hatred toward some members of the congregation for supporting TVA and the damn. There was that County Commissioner, she noticed, walking by to take his seat. How could he not sympathize with these families? What about Christ's admonition to "Do unto others as you would have them do unto you."

Suddenly the sound of organ interrupted her thoughts and she tried to focus on the worship service but noticed Myrtle Graham, sitting alone in a pew that used to be full of family. Myrtle was the widow of Bill Graham who some believed had died from the stress produced by TVA.

Neil had purchased a special ring from a mountain craftsman. It was a band of gold, rimmed in silver, containing a cluster of small stones, a diamond in the center flanked by two birthstones, his on one side and Tish's on the other. It was not at all ostentatious, even if he could have afforded a bigger diamond, he knew what Tish liked. At least, he hoped he knew because he was ready to ask the question, but he couldn't decide where or when.

It was getting closer and closer to Christmas and Neil was running out of time. His parents were coming within the next couple of days. Tish was busy helping her mother prepare for all their expected guests. He decided he'd phone Tish and make some plans.

"Hello," Tish answered.

"When can we get together? I need to see you before all the family and friends get here and get us all tangled up in their doings."

"If you're not busy, why don't you come over right now. I could use your help. We've decided to string lights on the barn for the first time. "

"Aren't you afraid of fire?" Neil was concerned.

"Oh, we won't leave them plugged in, They'll be lighted only for a short time, kind of a welcome for the visitors, and we'll keep a close watch, even then."

"I see," he said. "I imagine they will like that."

This was not what Neil was hoping for but he supposed he would have to go along if he expected to see Tish. He changed into a clean set of barn clothes, putting the ring deep into his pocket and jumped into his truck. He drove to the Jamison place and saw Tish on a ladder leaned against the front of the barn.

She smiled brightly, "Glad you're here. I'm afraid I might break my neck on this ladder; it's kind of rickety."

Neil convinced Tish to string the lights only over the hallway entrance at the front of the barn and to add a sprig of mistletoe to the center. Immediately after the task was accomplished, he took her in his arms and kissed her, a long, lingering passionate kiss. Just as he was about to take the ring out of his pocket and pop the question, he heard a whistle. It came from Tish's Uncle Jack.

"Wow!" Uncle Jack teased, "It's broad daylight; aren't you two afraid of the rumor mill?"

Neil and Tish laughed, then Neil said, "Everybody already knows about us, so what's there to say!" Although Neil hadn't initially planned to propose in the barn, he was tired of waiting for a special time, so he had planned to go ahead today and was disappointed that Jack had ruined his moment.

The three of them admired the lights, then left for the house. As soon as Jack walked through the door, Neil stopped and asked Tish, "Do you want to go out tonight and have dinner with me?"

"I'd love to but I can't, I promised Mamma that I would help her grind stuff for her famous cranberry salad. You know, Christmas Eve is day after tomorrow and we've got to prepare for about 30 or 40 people. I've lost count. "

"I see," Neil said, shaking his head in defeat, then had a thought. "If I come over after supper, will you be through by then?"

"I think so," Tish said.

"All right, I'll come over and we can see how the lights at the barn look after dark. Is that a deal?"

"Fine, I'll see you then." Tish strode into the house waving as she walked, feeling a little flutter in her stomach. He could still manage to stir up those butterflies, she realized.

Neil spent the rest of the day automatically doing the routine chores, visualizing his plans for the night ahead. After he was back inside his house, he made himself a sandwich, got dressed, shaved and waited until time to go. He found himself looking at his watch and then, out of the window, wishing it would go ahead and get dark.

Inside the kitchen at the Jamison home, Tish was busy working the old antique grinder that was currently attached to the kitchen table. She was grinding a bowl of unpeeled red apples that followed the oranges, nuts, cranberries, and celery, already ground into little pieces and placed into a giant bowl. The apples were the last of the ingredients. Her mother had a row of Pyrex dishes lined up on the counter plus a few molds, already containing the bright red gelatin liquid. As soon as Tish finished the apples, they would be added to the big bowl and then spooned into the gelatin. It was going to take a lot of salad to feed the crew coming tomorrow. Rebecca hoped she hadn't made a mistake in measuring the liquid because these salads were going to have to congeal overnight.

Finally, the whir of the hand cranking grinder stopped and mother and daughter worked together to complete their task and carry the dishes carefully to the extra refrigerator in the pantry just off the kitchen. Most farm families had to have more than one refrigerator, no matter how large.

Rebecca gave her daughter a hug, "Thank you, LaTisha, I could never have done it all without your help."

Tish hugged her mother back, "You know, you could scale back a little and ask everyone to bring a dish. You know, make it pot luck. Or get Dad to buy some of the stuff already prepared or even hire a caterer."

"But then, it wouldn't be Christmas like we all know it." Rebecca said.

They heard a knocking at the door.

Tish smiled and said, "I bet that's Neil and I look a mess, but we're just going to the barn to see how the lights look in the dark." She hurried to the door, taking off the old fashioned apron as she went and flinging it over the back of a chair. She knew she smelled of apples and wiped a tiny bit of peel from her face. She did not realize that her wild walnut hair had started to fall from the bun she had pinned it in.

 "Hello," Neil said when she opened the door. "Are you ready to go see how the lights look in the dark?"

"I suppose I should help clean up our mess . . ."

"Go ahead, honey," her mother interjected, "You've done enough."

Tish smiled gratefully and left with Neil. "Let's just walk to the barn. No sense in driving such a short distance." As they walked, he put his arm around her waist and she his, and they walked in unison. The temperature was dropping but it was still not cold, or at least, they didn't think so.

Inside the barn, Tish flipped the switch and they walked back out to admire the lights. The sparkling array of multi-colors gave the barn hall an inviting celebratory look and caused the mistletoe to glow. Neil pulled Tish back under it and wrapped his arms around her pulling her close to him." Now, I'm going to finish what I started earlier today before your Uncle Jack interrupted us." He kissed her and she felt herself swoon as the butterflies lifted in a flutter. Then, still standing under the mistletoe, he pulled the little box from his pocket and, looking into her eyes, asked the question that had been burning in his mind, "LaTisha Jamison, will you marry me?"

She looked back up at him and almost shouted,

"Yes!"

The horses, now awake from the new reflected light and sounds, began to nicker as if questioning what was happening. Neil and Tish laughed as he led her inside the barn where they fell into a pile of hay from broken bales.

They returned to the house and told Tish's mother who was still in the kitchen. She then went into the den and told Tish's father who came out and shook hands with his future son-in-law. Then phone calls were made. And, the grapevine was busy. News traveled fast in Jensen's Valley.

"No, we haven't set a date. No, we haven't decided where. Give us a little time just to enjoy our engagement."

The rest of the season passed in a wonderful blur as Tish and Neil celebrated Christmas with their families. When Neil's parents arrived, they had no idea they would be meeting their future daughter-in-law because Neil had kept the news as a surprise. Everyone, or so it seemed, had a suggestion for the wedding, as to when and where and how it should take place. This was especially true of Tish's sisters, but Tish had her own plans which she was not yet willing to share. Also, they were not going to be in a hurry because they had plenty of tasks to accomplish before they could live together. Tish's cottage was too small for the two of them and not close enough to Neil's beloved horses. His place could hardly be called furnished, with only the kitchen appliances, a table, a few chairs and two beds; that was pretty much it. They would move some of Tish's furniture, but most of it, she felt, would be out of place in the old farmhouse. She had a vision of how she wanted it to look and planned to haunt flea markets and antique shops for items she could refinish or paint.

Although Kat was happy for both Tish and Neil, she worried that Tish would not have time to help her establish a new publication in the area. Since she was still learning about the valley and the surrounding mountains, she felt she needed input from people she trusted, like her new friends, Tish and Julie. Her parents could help to an extent but they did not know all the people that Tish knew nor were they cognizant of the multiple layers of culture, from the historic early settler influences to modern mainstream life. These differences extended high into the mountains and spilled into the fertile fields of the valley floor. Tish's previous experience as a social worker had given her real insight into numerous facets of life in the area. Kat was trying to learn from Tish and she knew her education was not yet complete.

10
SNAIL DARTER MAKES LIST

It was a happy day for all the dam-resistors throughout the valley when the U.S. Department of Interior granted the listing of the snail darter as an endangered species and also determined the shoals of the river as critical habitat. But almost immediately, the media, both local and national, decided to go berserk over the fact that a tiny fish with an unattractive name had stopped a dam which had already been built. The network news anchors filled the television screens, touting the millions of dollars that had already been spent. They mocked the entire environmentalist movement and interviewed proponents of the project and TVA personnel who sneered at the so-called tree-huggers with contempt. Not much was said about the 500 plus tracts of land which had either already been seized or were about to be taken. TVA also defied the request of Tennessee's popular Governor Winfield Dunn, a Republican, who asked that the project be nixed, the Little T saved and the farmland spared. They knew Tennessee state law prevented the Governor from seeking reelection and flaunted the desires of the federal government over the wishes of the state.

In 1976, although in Federal Court District Judge Robert T. Taylor finds TVA guilty of seven violations of the Endangered Species Act, he nevertheless refused to file a stop-work injunction. As a result, TVA increased the speed of its ongoing destruction of the valley and cut the huge old river beeches at Coytee Springs where the Cherokee Indians had signed a treaty knowing this picturesque and historic site was not going to be under water. Even as this act of defiance demoralized the opponents, they continued to fight.

Before launching a new publication, Kat had to find a place to work. There were plenty of vacant buildings to choose from. She chose to rent a small old storefront space in Jensen's Valley and created an office for her new periodical, the *Valley Gazette.* She managed to hire Tish to work as an assistant, helping in a variety of tasks. Although Tish had been helping in her father's office some, filling in when his secretary went on vacation or wanted some time off, she remained unemployed and was searching for what she should do in the future. She did enjoy helping Neil with the horses in his care, so she was never at a loss for things to do, but helping with the *Gazette* was something that needed to be done.

Setting up the office was an enjoyable task after Tish and Kat cajoled Julie into helping them paint the interior. They laughed at each other when it looked as though they had gotten more paint on themselves than on the walls, but the end result was acceptable. The Scotts found and contributed enough excess furniture which had been stored on the estate to furnish the office. It looked stylish, really, Kat thought as she looked around the office of her new publishing venture. She had won awards for journalistic excellence and, although they were displayed in the office of her former employers, she had hung copies of them, graciously provided by her old boss. She had also framed and hung her college degree. These were displayed in an effort to give her new little paper credibility among the citizens.

All of the opponents to the project who lived in or near the valley quickly discovered the new local publication that presented their point of view. They became subscribers and wrote letters to the editor which Kat gratefully published. She also published a few samples of hate mail which revealed the ignorance of some of the proponents who spouted like parrots some of the rhetoric used by the Charles Hall/Red Wagner faction. But, reaching far more people was the *Knoxville Journal* which continued to present in a fair and unbiased manner the controversial story of the fight to save the river. They, unlike Knoxville's other major newspaper, the *Knoxville News-Sentinel*, did not fold under pressure from TVA although they did pay a price in lost revenue. At times, Kat wondered if her publication was even needed since the *Journal* was doing its job, but Tish and Julie as well as others reminded her that the other papers in the area tried to convey the message that all local people wanted the lake. *The Tri-County Observer* in Madisonville and the *Loudon County Herald* and the *Lenoir City News Banner* were all enjoying the advertising money from Hall's Telephone Company, and the so-called movers and shakers who wanted something, anything, other than a farming community.

Although the citizens had welcomed and appreciated the paper, there just weren't enough of them to make much of a financial impact. Also, many small businesses were short of funds due to the loss of customers who had been forced to migrate to parts unknown. Without customers, there wasn't much need to buy advertising. The established paper was being supported by TVA and their boosters who kept promising prosperity and a big boon of business just as soon as the valley was flooded.

Tish helped Kat promote the *Gazette*, wishing she and her paper had been around a decade earlier when it might have made a difference locally, but now, both Loudon and Vonore were towns that seemed to be dying and taking Jensen's Valley along with it. If they were not dying altogether, they were changing from the stable, pretty little towns that were so well loved by many into a questionable future.

Loudon, the county seat, was not so little prior to the building of the dam. It had a diverse economy, agriculture and industry, including a number of manufacturing plants. Many local youngsters were able to find jobs following their high school graduation in any number of plants. The economy was by no means all agriculture, but the farming community was very significant in the amount of revenues brought into the region.

Because the Department of Interior had put the snail darter and its critical habitat on the Endangered Species List, the opponents of the project were no longer only landowners or history buffs or sportsmen but environmentalists from all over the country. They had standing to file an appeal of Judge Taylor's ruling that permitted work on the project to continue.

TVA evicted more than families. All the churches and cemeteries within the water-line had to be moved. Members of Union Fork Baptist Church were informed during a Sunday Service on a bright, sunlit morning which glazed the headstones in their adjoining cemetery that TVA was rushing them to act. They had found property to relocate on a lot adjacent to the new Highway 72 which would go from Loudon to Hwy 411 between Vonore and Madisonville.

One family whose relatives would have to be moved from their final resting place remarked to Kat, "Those real estate folks are thrilled, aren't they? They're selling lots, not only to the living but also to the dead. Why, you can almost hear the jingle in their pockets because of all this moving about, some of it at the taxpayers' expense, most of it going straight to TVA and their cronies."

Kat nodded; saddened that so many pretty places were going to be drowned.

She had enjoyed the drive on old Vonore Road to Union Fork Creek Cemetery. It was a scenic one, especially the Bacon Farm, situated along the Little T. A vast expansion of lawn dotted with numerous old shade trees with white-painted trunks cascaded from the sprawling house. The barns were equally impressive.

Old Colonel Bacon had been dead for years, but he was still a fixture in Loudon and the county. Many places had been named for him, mainly because he had been the force behind various businesses and a major contributor to community projects. There was the Bacon Creamery, Bacon Hosiery Mill, and Bacon Hospital where he spent his final days. He left no children and as his friends and associates passed away, few would know what all he had accomplished. Kat made a mental note to research his life and write a story about him. She has already learned that he had generated his own electricity on his farm from a creek which ran into the Little T long before TVA operated in the area. The milking machines in his dairy barn were powered by this electricity. Milk from his cows, along with that from other dairies, was processed by the creamery he established. She had also learned that he was quite wealthy. Most people who managed to make a fortune had led interesting lives and she imagined his life would be too. Yes, that would be a story.

One day after passing the bar exam, University of Tennessee student Hank Hill and a little band of young lawyers, Zyg Plater, Peter Alliman, and three others loaded into a Toyota truck with a camper on the bed and drove to Cincinnati to file an appeal in the Sixth

Circuit Court of Appeals. Since Judge Taylor had found violations, he should have issued an injunction to stop work. They knew the law, but could they prevail in a politically charged environment. They didn't know, but they felt they had to try.

As young advocates, they were hard pressed for money; the diminished number of landowners also had diminished funds from the ongoing fight with the giant, super powerful TVA, and had little to give the lawyers, so they were forced to travel in the most cost-effective way possible. It was a cold night and they got very little sleep in the back of the pick-up truck. It was too small for all of them, so some of them tried to sleep in the front seat, but found it impossible to stay asleep for long. Hank kept bumping his head on the steering wheel, waking himself. They had planned to alternate drivers and drive all night, but became too sleepy and had to pull over beside the highway. Tall, lanky Zyg, stretched out in the back, kept turning and poking the others who were lying cramped alongside him. It is no wonder that they woke early on that January 31 morning and sought shelter in a restaurant where they gulped coffee. It was nerves and excitement that kept them awake until time for the hearing.

Meanwhile, TVA lawyers, having flown in on an eight passenger jet, were rested, dressed to impress, and moved with an arrogant attitude into the courtroom. Once they settled themselves with great show into their seats to await the judge, they glanced across the room and appeared to sneer at opposing counsel. Inside the room, Hank Hill, the plaintiff, represented by Zygmunt Plater and the little entourage of fellow students together managed to look presentable if not overly impressive.

Although they did not have to wait long, their nerves and fatigue made it seem like an interminable amount of time. Finally, the Appellate Judge, Anthony Calebreeze, heard their appeal and sided with the young, upstart lawyers and ruled the project could not be completed. Furthermore, he ordered a permanent injunction to halt work on the project.

They were ecstatic. Hill smiled and slapped Plater and Alliman on the back. The unthinkable had actually happened. Someone ruled against the giant and powerful government agency!

The so-called big shots with TVA and Wagner were furious with Judge Calebreeze. When they heard the ruling, Wagner turned as red as his hair and began pacing. How dare the judge go against them! Didn't the Calebreeze know who he was up against! Quickly, without any discussion, TVA instructed their attorneys to file an appeal to the U.S. Supreme Court. He'd show them, he thought, his face remaining as red as his hair, what was left of it. These tree-huggers, as he called them, were making him go bald. He was confident he'd win when the Supremes heard the case. After all, TVA was government, and they had 82 lawyers currently on their payroll.

Following the ruling, TVA workers parked their giant earth-moving machines and walked away, leaving them in place. There was not much more land clearing left to do, but they would have to demolish the homes of the hold-outs after the Supreme Court overturned the Sixth Circuit's ruling, at least that's what they were told by their superiors. Wagner was appalled that Zyg Plater was still working with those students who got these lawsuits started. He thought when his friends had gotten Plater fired from the University of Tennessee for spending too much time on the Tellico project, that he'd be free from the likes of him and his followers. His only worry was that some of the justices on the Court were Nixon appointees. And Nixon, blast him, was responsible for that Endangered Species Act in the first place. But, Nixon's reputation had been ruined, thanks to Senator Baker, a new kind of Republican, was one of TVA's most dependable supporters. And, the Democrats were back in charge of Tennessee government. Most always in favor of big government, the Democrats had never failed to support TVA, no matter what they said in their campaigns. So, Wagner was guardedly optimistic and pushed on with his ever changing propaganda, making fun of the tree-hugger mentalities and especially the little fish standing in the way of progress. There was a plethora of jokes about the little snail darter stopping the so-called important project.

The landowners were jubilant. Although most had already moved, they were happy that the hold-outs could stay, at least until the Supreme Court heard the case. The remaining landowners had already been condemned earlier through the law of eminent domain, but had refused to accept the money even though TVA had deposited into their bank accounts.

The hold outs ignored the money and stayed in their homes on their property. Now, they had real hope, even as they lived in limbo, that they might actually be able to avoid eviction.

While the landowners and residents of the valley waited to find out what would ultimately happen, an unknown person or persons added levity to the situation by sneaking around the security guards that were assigned to various areas near the dam and TVA's vast arsenal of equipment leaving graffiti. The graffiti always left the same message, "Scarecrow was here."

Newspaper reporters took photographs of the white signature messages scrawled across TVA bulldozers which were parked at various sites. The public was amused but TVA was embarrassed when the photographs were published. It became almost a serial in the papers as episodically another incident was recorded, a different machine but the same message. It even appeared on the dam itself, giving some opponents hope that the dreaded dam could perhaps be blown up. A little vandalism occurred, nothing much, no major damage, just some action to let the public and TVA know that the Scarecrow had been there. Sometimes gears were shifted or a big machine was moved slightly. People began to speculate as to who the Scarecrow could be, but he was not telling anyone, at least, no one reported having been told. Some thought perhaps he was a disgruntled employee because not everyone within TVA thought it was fair to take one person's land and profit by selling it to another.

One day, Julie confided to Tish, "I think my Jimmy

is the scarecrow."

"Why? Would he not tell you?" Tish asked.

"I don't think he would trust me to keep my mouth shut. He'd know, of course, that I wouldn't get him in trouble on purpose, but I'd just have to tell the people I trust, and you know how that goes, they'd tell others until the wrong person found out."

"Well, what makes you think it's him?"

"Because he makes his living using equipment like the kind TVA is using. He would know how to do those things the scarecrow does, shift gears, roll backwards, you know, take a bolt or screw."

"Well, I have wondered myself who it could be, but I just hope they don't catch him, whoever he is because I'm sure TVA would try to throw the book at him. Do you think some of the security guards just look the other way? He's left so many messages in so many different places, looks like one of them would have seen him. We are assuming it is a man, but it could be a woman or a couple of teenagers."

"Wonder if we'll ever know," Julie mused, then said softly, "If it is Jimmy, I guess he'll tell me eventually."

11
THE WEDDING

Neil and Tish were tired of waiting to share a home together. They had been unsuccessful in getting Tish's little terrier to bond with Neil's Border collie. Every time they got them together, each dog seemed to be trying to defend its territory, growling and threatening the other.

"I don't know much about dog-training," Neil said. "If they were horses, I'd know what to do."

"I've been thinking about leaving Tyke with my Dad. He loves to go over there and seems really happy when I leave him with them, which I have always done when I'm away, like on trips. That way, I can still be with him when I want to but I won't have to worry about him getting chewed up by your protector." Tish said.

"I don't want you to give up your dog. I'm sure there's a way we could make them get along."

"Maybe we'll figure it out, but meanwhile, I'll leave him with my folks, because I'm tired of us having to maintain two places and traipse back and forth like illicit lovers, aren't you?

"Absolutely!" Neil's smile was enthusiastic. He had been eager to marry Tish for a long time and was tired of waiting, not knowing exactly how and when they were finally going to be married. "Have you decided how and when you want us to tie the knot?"

"Yes," Tish answered, her voice subdued, "but you might not like it."

"I've told you before, any time, any place . . . I just want you." Neil stroked her cheeks and kissed her softly, eager to hear her plans.

"Well, as you know, the river and the valley are in limbo waiting to see what happens. While we still have it, free-flowing like it is, I'd like to get married on a boat floating down the Little T. I believe the Steele boys still have a boat we can rent. All we would have to do is get a preacher and a couple of witnesses to float down with us. We could put in somewhere at a take-out and have a little reception. What do you think?"

"I think it's a great idea, mainly because it can happen quickly."

"But what about your parents, Neil, will they be upset if we don't have a more traditional wedding?"

"No, I don't think so. But, what about yours?"

"I think they will be relieved. I remember what an ordeal it was when my sisters got married. Mother was younger then, but she was still stressed out with all the preparation, having to attend teas and showers. If I were the only daughter, maybe she'd want me to have a big wedding, but she's been through it twice already. I think she'll be relieved, really."

So, it was decided. All they had to do was find a preacher who would be willing. Fortunately, Neil had an old friend who had gone into the ministry. He was currently the pastor of a non-denominational Christian church on the outskirts of Nashville. As boys, the two of them had been close, but college had separated them and sent them in different directions. Neil wasn't sure if Max would be willing, but he was going to call and find out. Max was definitely his first choice.

One of the Steele brothers would handle the boat and could also be a witness, but Tish wanted Julie to be her maid of honor. If she had only one sister, she would feel obligated to ask her, but since she had two, neither of whom would like her choice of a wedding site, she was going to ask Julie. And, perhaps Neil would ask Julie's husband Jimmy since they had become good friends. Wonder how many people the boat could accommodate? Better limit the number to just the essential people.

"After the ceremony, we'll arrange to put in on land that is still private property, or at least some that TVA has not already taken over, and have our car there. Then we can attend a little reception wherever our folks choose to have it. What do you think?

"Great!"

Later, it was decided that the reception would be held by the river near where the boat would unload the wedding party. Although the owners of the land had received their eviction notice, the transfer had not taken place. The lovely and stately old home, located near the river, slightly upstream from the take-out point, would provide the caterers with a kitchen and the guests access to a bathroom. It was going to be perfect, but also, a little sad for the owners who knew that the place was soon going to be taken from them if TVA got its way. The wedding reception would perhaps be the last event held at their place.

Exactly three weeks later, during the last week of June, Neil and Tish were to be married. Neil's friend Max had been happy when asked to come and conduct the ceremony, saying he had always wanted to float the famous Little T. He agreed to come a couple of days early so that he and Neil could catch up on each other's activities and reminisce about their childhood escapades. Tish liked Max immediately as did everyone who met him, especially Kat.

Tish rose early on the morning of her wedding day, had coffee with her mother and sisters in the familiar kitchen and watched with pleasure the dawn light shimmer gradually through the window panes to dance across their coffee cups.

"Looks like the weathermen were right," her mother said, "it's starting out to be a beautiful day. You know the old saying, 'Red sky at night, sailors delight, red sky in the morning, sailors warning.' Well, I don't see a bit of red in this sunrise, just a bright yellow glow."

Tish dressed in a white sundress and pinned a floppy, wide-brimmed hat into her hair which had been arranged on top of her head. I hope the hat doesn't blow away, she thought, adding some additional hairpins to secure both her hairdo and the hat more securely. She carried a bouquet of wild flowers which one of her sisters described as being made of plain old blooming weeds. Tish didn't care what they were. She thought they were pretty and remembered picking them as a child while playing "house" and "here comes the bride" and other make-believe games of the past.

The trip down the river was like magic to them. They put the boat in during an early morning hour so they could enjoy the special flickering sunlight on the water. As they passed various landmarks, including areas where TVA had bulldozed and destroyed the vegetation along the banks, Neil was fearful that Tish might regret her decision to have their wedding on the river. It was sad to see the battle scars of the valley and river that had been inflicted by TVA. Tish chose to think about the possibility of nature reclaiming all that was lost. Nothing was going to stop her from cherishing the day. She focused on the fast water beneath them, able to see fish through the clear stream carrying them along. It was a grand experience for Max who had never been to the area. Jimmy and Julie relayed some points of history, explaining where various Cherokee towns had been located. Then, too quickly, it seemed to Max, it was time for the couple to exchange their vows. Max stood before them as the boat was steered nearer the shoreline, placing them on a shoal of calmer water. Neil and Tish faced each other and made the time-honored pledges straight out of the

King James Bible. Max pronounced them man and wife. Neil grabbed Tish, kissed her, and shouted to the wind, "married at last!" Everyone was all smiles as congratulatory hugs were given. Jimmy and Julie held hands and looked at each other as they exchanged a quick kiss.

"Pretty romantic, wasn't it?" Julie commented.

"Yes, do you want a do-over since we did our thing in the courthouse?" Jimmy asked, a little worried that Julie might have regrets about their no-frills civil ceremony.

Julie gave him an impish smile and said, "I'll think about it, but I'm satisfied with the husband I got that day."

The boating party then floated the rest of the way down the river to the take-out point where the reception was waiting for them. As they approached, they could hear the music being played by Emmett Moss and the Crazy Creek band. There were others from the mountain community, people who had shared such a significant part of Tish's life. And, as she looked about, it was as if just about everyone from both the mountain and the valley communities were there. Tears formed in her eyes. She was so blessed to have such fine friends as those gathered there, especially the people who had already been evicted and forced to move away. They had returned for her wedding, in spite of the sadness they must feel. And, Neil had invited numerous people from Middle Tennessee in addition to his parents and relatives.

The food was spread out on the tables as a line formed to greet the couple before they moved on to be served with abundant portions from the numerous dishes. What looked like a small tent city also featured a bar with numerous kinds of wine and punch, some with alcohol and some without.

Neil and Tish were ecstatic, so glad the weather had cooperated. They greeted everyone warmly and Tish was given a bear hug by Emmett. They had shared more adventure than many in a lifetime so Emmett was especially fond of Tish as was his entire family and, she was equally fond of him. The sun was now high and shedding warmer and warmer rays. It was time for the couple to leave. No one knew exactly where they were going. Pa Ferguson, with the help of Jason Webb, was going to take care of the horses and the farm while they were away.

The couple waved good-bye amid the bubbles blown by the onlookers, and they were off, but not before Tish had thrown her bouquet to Kat. It was little, made with a trailing length of ivy added to the wildflower mix, and was a little weather- beaten from wind on the river, but it had held together. Kat caught it and smiled. She hoped that someday she too would meet Mister Right as her sister had before her untimely death. She thought of her sister's fiancée whom she had never met and wondered how he had gotten on with his life. She also found herself wishing that Max lived closer because there was something about him . . . but, he was a minister and she had never hung out with a man of the cloth, she mused, before pushing the thoughts away, thinking it was just because of Tish and Neil's wedding that she was more aware of being single and alone. Yet, she was having fun with the local fellow who was always the life of the party, Roger Kinealy. Although she had been warned by both Tish and Julie to watch out for him because he was known to be what they called "a womanizer of the dangerous sort."

The newlyweds had decided to drive down the Natchez Trace to the coast and return by some other route. They would travel on and off the trace, visiting various places along the way, staying a few days in Natchez, then driving along the coast through Mobile, Gulf Shores and finally through Georgia back home in Tennessee. It was something they had both wanted to do and now seemed to be as good a time as any. Mainly, they just wanted to be together without any responsibilities.

"I don't want to see an animal of any kind," Neil said, "unless it's wild. You know how much I love those horses and all the other critters on the farm, but they sure are demanding."

"I know what you mean, I sure will be happy to see Ginger when we get back, but it's going to be great not to have to feed anything but ourselves!"

Meanwhile, in the valley, a summer heat wave moved in from the West and engulfed the area, climbing even into the mountains. As the temperature rose, so did the humidity and together, they made the afternoons quite miserable.

"About the only place to get cool outside of air-conditioning is in the Little T," Jimmy remarked and winked at Julie. He had been going to work at dawn, but knocking off at noon. It was just too hot to run the machines in the afternoon.

"I hope it's not this hot where Tish and Neil are," Julie said.

"Oh, I'll bet it's hot, wherever they are, inside or out," Jimmy said, teasingly, and reached over grabbing Julie and pulling her to him, "Remember, they are on their honeymoon!"

At the farm, Rebecca was finally able to rest. Although she loved seeing all the family and friends that had poured in for the wedding, she was exhausted. Her older daughters had helped her, but she continued to experience the stress of feeling the responsibility for everyone's well-being.

Their garden had yielded well all summer, beginning with early spring peas and onions and radishes, followed by squash and green beans, and cucumbers. Finally, the tomatoes which had hung on green so long had begun to ripen. It was nice to be able to live on tomato sandwiches for a while and not have to cook.

The only downside had been the corn and cantaloupes which the raccoons had checked out and found ready to pick. They ate them all; it looked the same as if a person had pulled the ears off the cornstalks. The varmints didn't bother to take the melons off the vine, they just ate them where they lay, leaving only the rinds of what had been perfectly ripe and ready to eat cantaloupes.

"I should shoot every raccoon I see," Charles said, shaking his head.

"No, you know you can't," Rebecca said, "they are just so cute, and you're as tender-hearted as the rest of us, but you can trap them and take them up the mountain or somewhere, anywhere away from here. I think TVA has run them out of their old homes. Next, we'll be getting deer and bears down here."

It was still early in the morning as they walked to the side porch from the garden carrying baskets of the tomatoes they had gathered to place on the window seal.

"I love fresh produce from the garden and always enjoy seeing things grow, but I'm just too tired to can and freeze this summer." Rebecca sank back on the chaise lounge as Charles dropped into the rocking chair beside her. A small fountain with a cherub and a frog spewing water was located just outside the screened porch. As the water fell onto the small rocks piled into the bottom, it made soothing sounds reminiscent of mountain streams.

"Well, dear, now that we've gotten our last daughter married off, maybe we can retire and enjoy ourselves. When Tish and Neil get back, do you want to take a trip? We haven't been anywhere in ages."

"I'll think about it. Right now, I don't have the energy to pack."

"I think it's time you saw a doctor. It's not like you to be so tired. I know you have been pushing yourself.

You've probably just overdone it, but it wouldn't hurt to get checked out."

"We'll see. Right now, I think I'll settle down with a good book. You know, I love to read and haven't had time lately."

Kat was staying busy with her newspaper. The residents of the valley seemed to appreciate the little publication. They suggested features and shared their concerns as well as successes. When anyone won a competition or a child won a prize, it was reported with an accompanying photo and the family bought extra papers to clip from, for scrap books, and sometimes to mail to distant relatives. Life continued on, but hanging like a dark shadow behind all the everyday activities was the continuing threat of TVA drowning the valley. The feeling hung like a dark cloak over the place, causing people to shudder from its feeling of darkness and gloom.

As the subscriptions grew, Kat hired some part-time help which made her busy life more bearable. No one seemed to know how much work was involved to put out a paper.

"The words don't just jump on the page and print themselves," she remarked to Julie one day when she was being chastised for working all the time.

"I know," Julie said, "but you don't have to kill yourself. Hire some people."

"I want the newspaper to make a profit, not go further in debt."

"If I were you, and didn't have to work, I wouldn't work at all."

"But, I do have to work. I can't just live off my parents," Kat responded.

She wrote some fascinating features, like the story about the bloodhounds who tracked James Earl Ray after he escaped from Brushy Mountain Prison. The hounds were trained and owned by a man named Meeks who lived in McMinn County. They were beautiful dogs, with friendly eyes, long, floppy ears, and tongues lolling out of their mouths, seeming to smile at Kat as she snapped photos of them.

She covered horse shows and mule shows and parades, political events, and just about everything people in the small towns cared about or participated in. She actually found herself fascinated with Sessions Court which was held in a small but crowded room at the jail. It was to determine whether some of the people arrested or ticketed would be held over for the grand jury or instead fined, charged with a misdemeanor and let go with a tongue lashing from the judge.

Although domestic violence was serious and nothing to be made fun of, Kat could not stop herself from laughing when a wife admitted that she had struck her husband over the head with a frying pan when she discovered lipstick on the collar of his shirt. A shouting match had followed that incident with the sheriff being called by neighbors and charges filed. Now, both husband and wife stood before the judge, embarrassed and anxious about what he would do.

He glared at them, "Either get a divorce or get along. I am fining you $100 and I don't want to see you in here again. If there is a next time, I'll lock you up!

Both of you!" He continued his famous threatening glare in silence before saying, "Next."

The judge moved along quickly, from necessity because the docket was long, primarily traffic violations including DUI, trespassing, hunting out of season, theft, and drug-related charges which included growing, possession and selling marijuana. It seemed that marijuana had replaced moonshine as the most dominant illegal product in the area. The arrests of moonshiners had become very rare. It was as though the process of making liquor had become almost a lost art. One former mountain distiller said the process of making 'shine involved too much work for the modern generation. It was easier to plant marijuana plants and just watch them grow.

12
IN LIMBO

When Neil and Tish returned from their honeymoon, they resumed their daily ritual of taking care of the horses. Neil had to catch up with the ones he had in training. With two of the young ones, it was like starting all over. He was bucked off one of them before he even got settled in the saddle. He got up, dusted himself off and moved around to make sure his limbs were still intact. It was if he had been away much longer than the week and two days that they were gone.

"That'll remind me to lunge you before I get on. I'm afraid you are a cold-backed son of a gun. Not good news for your owner, I'm afraid." He clipped a lunge line to the halter and began working the horse in the round pen. Around and around the horse went, exhibiting an excess of pent-up energy. Neil had him change directions and move in the other direction around the pen, watching the horse for signals of acceptance. Finally, the horse began to move his lips and demonstrate in the sign language that horses use, that he was perhaps willing to be ridden. Contrary to what some so-called expert trainers said, this sign of acceptance did not guarantee that the rider would not be tossed into the air again. Neil knew from experience, there was no sure thing with horses, no rule that couldn't be broken by them, only indicators.

He allowed the big gelding to approach him. They communicated ever so carefully as Neil decided it was time for him to climb back on. Taking advantage of his long legs, he swung into the saddle quickly. This time, the horse was cooperative and moved as directed, turning this way and that as Neil sought to soften his muscles, turning the horse's neck around one way and then the other. They then moved into a trot around the pen.

"Good boy," Neil spoke soothingly as he rode and could feel the big roan settle beneath him.

Meanwhile, Tish was in the kitchen preparing lunch. She had fried some bacon and was slicing tomatoes from her parent's garden to make bacon and tomato sandwiches. She had made a big pitcher of sweet iced tea. When Neil walked in, she noticed that he appeared to be limping a little.

"What's wrong," she asked, "your gait is off a little," she tried to joke but was concerned.

"Oh, old Buck threw me, but I'm all right, just a little sore."

"Who is old Buck? Have you named one I don't know about?"

"Well, yes, that two-year old roan I've got in training for that yuppie in Knoxville. Since he threw me, I decided I might as well call him Buck while he's here. I know that's not real original as a name, but it'll do while he's here. I don't remember what his owner called him if he mentioned a name. I don't believe he did. He's probably got a registered name from the AQHA."

"I hope he's the only bad one you have to train. That's the trouble when you take one in from somewhere else. And, especially those quarter horses. I think most of them are rowdier than the Tennessee Walkers, don't you?"

"Maybe, but it really depends on the individual horse." Neil answered.

"You don't know anything about how they were treated before they got here." Tish said, going over to Neil and rubbing his shoulders. She placed a big glass of tea by his plate and proceeded to make a sandwich for him.

"I'm getting spoiled," Neil said, "I always had to make my own sandwiches before. I think I like having a wife."

"You better like me for more than my sandwiches," she laughed.

"After I finish this, you'll see what else I like!" Neil said, "Our honeymoon wasn't near long enough."

* * *

There were three property owners, or four if one counted Tom Miller who owned a house but not the land it sat on, land rented back from the Carsons, who leased it back from TVA. They continued to occupy their homes. The three landowners vowed they would never leave voluntarily but Miller was willing to move his house whenever TVA told him to go. If the lawsuit saved the river, then he wouldn't have to go at all.

Eighty-five year old Nellie McCall was one of the last hold-outs. She blamed TVA for the death of her husband, Asa McCall. The elderly couple was devoted to their 90-acre Greenback farm and the life they had shared there. Everyone who knew Asa believed it was the stress of the condemnation notice that caused his death. It was Asa who had passed the hat to collect funds to file the lawsuit using the newly found snail darter and the Endangered Species Act as defense of the river. Now, he was gone and unless he could see down from heaven, he wouldn't know the outcome. But Nellie believed he could see and would know, so she was going to stay put.

Some of the farmers who had already sold their land to TVA were able to rent it back to farm while the various legal issues continued. Still other farmers who had not owned any land were also able to lease acreage to take advantage of the rich soils to grow corn, soybeans and other row crops. It did seem a shame to not use the productive land before it was covered with water. And, many acres above the flood line but within the taking line would never see a drop of lake water, but belonged to TVA.

Tom Miller grew up on the banks of the river, the Little Tennessee, as the son of a renter who worked the land. He rode a mule across the river to school, carrying his lunch in a lard can. Tom loved the river and the valley. When TVA bought the Carson property for the project, Tom was able to buy a large brick house from John Carson. He planned to move the house, but when litigation halted work on the project, Carson leased his land back from TVA and subsequently, both Carson and TVA told Miller that he could keep the house on the land, pending the legal battle. In fact, it was a TVA attorney who suggested that Miller stay.

The Ritchey family continued farming their land, having returned the check TVA had mailed them. Later, they found TVA had deposited the money into their bank account. They ignored the money and continued living in the pretty farmhouse they loved.

And, Beryl Moser, the mailman who had been a member of the first group which met back in the 60's and organized the Association for the Preservation of the Little Tennessee River, was still hanging on to his family home and acreage in Vonore. He and the others hoped their diligence would be rewarded and they could stay.

Life continued as people in the valley remained in limbo, waiting. Winter came with a vengeance forcing people to stay inside for most of their days. Farm families, however, didn't have that luxury; they had to take care of the livestock, breaking ice on frozen troughs and ponds. Then, one morning, after Neil and Tish had finished taking care of the horses, they sat down in front of the fireplace with coffee to watch the morning news. Tish stiffened when she heard the reporter on a Knoxville television station announce that the murder trial of Alex Morgan would begin the following Monday in Athens. His defense attorney had argued for and was granted the change-of-venue. Still, Athens was not very far away. It was located in neighboring McMinn County. It was believed, however, that the jury pool there would not have a preconceived opinion about the guilt or innocence of Alex Morgan.

"I knew this day was coming, sometime," she said to Neil, "so I don't know why it's so upsetting."

"Oh, Honey, of course it's upsetting. He nearly killed you after murdering your best friend. You'll get through it, though. I'm sure he'll go back to prison." Neil tried to be reassuring.

"I just don't know why he didn't plead guilty to everything, not just to beating me up."

"Well," Neil said, "your dad and I both caught him in the act of assaulting you, so he had no defense at all. The only reason they didn't charge him with attempted murder then instead of just assault was because they thought you might die and if that happened, it wouldn't have been attempted murder, it would have been murder."

"I know that," Tish said, "but I heard him admit to killing Marlo. Don't people believe me?"

"Of course they do, but if you will remember, you were unconscious at the time and weren't able to tell anyone until you came to."

Meanwhile, in Pennsylvania where one of her brothers lived, Mary, Alex's ex-wife, had been able to find and rent a small house in a modest but decent neighborhood. Several of her neighbors had young children about the same age as her two sons. She certainly was not going to return to Tennessee to testify for Alex. He had been a deceitful, lying, cheating spouse who had left her heartbroken with the heavy burden of caring for their two young boys. Unfortunately, the boys still asked about their father, and poor Mary was unsure what she should say. She had taken the advice of her relatives and arranged for them to have counseling, hoping that the sessions would help them get through the sadness of the separation from their father and prepare them for the future.

The attorney who was defending Alex kept telephoning, putting pressure on her to attend the trial, but she was steadfast in her refusal, much to the chagrin of her brother-in-law who had hired the lawyer and was trying to assist in the defense. The attorney was also making demands that the boys be allowed to visit their father in prison which was another request that she continued to deny.

The phone rang and Mary picked it up. It was Alex's attorney. This time she shouted into the phone, "He was going to leave us, his sons and me, for Marlo. It was only because she rejected him that he now sends you begging. Well, I have no sympathy. Ever hear that quote, 'Hell hath no fury like a woman scorned?' Well, it's true because, if I could, I would flail him myself! I wish he would get the death penalty, but I've been told they're not even going to ask for it because the murder wasn't premeditated. So, what will he get, 20 or so years? It won't be enough, whatever it is. Good bye!" Mary slammed the phone back on the receiver.

She didn't understand all the legal mumbo jumbo, like the difference between First Degree and Second Degree Murder or Felony Murder, or whatever else they could choose to try him for. She didn't really care what charges sent him to prison. All she knew was that she hoped he would be locked up and out of her life and the lives of her children forever. She wanted to forget that he was their father.

Kat had never seen the man who had murdered her twin. She wasn't sure she could or should report the trial in her newspaper. Perhaps she would leave that story to the other publications because she could not be objective. She knew Alex was guilty of the murder because she trusted Tish completely and Tish had told her that Marlo had confessed to having an affair, of seeing Alex's shirt in her home, then, finally, Alex's admission as he was attacking her. Kat would attend the trial, however, out of morbid curiosity to see him, the man who had killed her sister. Also, she wanted to be supportive of her parents who would be in the courtroom out of a sense of duty to seek justice for their beloved daughter.

It was on a cold winter day in January when the trial was scheduled to begin. Everywhere the Scotts went, the media followed. People began arriving at the courthouse early that morning and long before the trial was to begin, the courtroom was filled to capacity.

Alex was sitting in a holding area with his attorney and his brother. Police officers were standing guard outside the door. Alex was nervous. Although he had been incarcerated for a little over a year, he had found himself often in denial of the consequences of his actions. When alone in his cell, he would often whisper to Marlo, saying to himself, "Why, why . . ." He thought sure he was going to have a life with her. How dare she turn on him like she had! Then, there was that hateful Tish . . . if only he hadn't gotten caught. His thoughts seemed to take his mind through a maze. Sometimes, he would wake from a dream, thinking that he was free, that his arrest never happened. Now he was disgraced and life would never be the same. Then he would become saddened and have some regret. His brother and the pastor had encouraged him to seek forgiveness from the Almighty. Alex, though, was praying all right, but he was praying for an acquittal.

"Everyone stand!"

The judge entered and motioned for the crowd to sit down. Kat had just entered the courtroom and happened to be standing against the wall. Since the room was full, she remained standing with some other reporters also there when Alex was brought into the room. Tish, seated with Neil and her father, noticed that Alex no longer had the cocky, yuppie expression on his face. His demeanor was now somewhat cowed. While she was looking at him, she noticed his eyes grow wild and he attempted to shake loose from the officers accompanying him. He had just spotted Kat and believed it was Marlo's ghost coming back to haunt him. While the officers grabbed him, he yelled, "Let me go!"

Some observers wondered if he was going to try to act insane to beat the charges, but Alex was not acting.

Perhaps he had lost touch with reality because he really believed it was Marlo standing there glaring at him from across the room.

He was almost dragged to face the judge who read the various charges against him.

"How do you plead," the judge asked.

"Guilty! I'm guilty!" Alex sobbed, "I'm sorry," he was shouting loudly as he turned his head and cast a furtive glance toward Kat.

There was a murmur from the crowd. His attorney and his brother stared at each other in disbelief at what had happened. Then, the prosecutor also looked their way, wondering what had just happened. All had expected a long and rather contentious trial.

"Thank you, dear Lord," Gloria sighed. She had dreaded the thought of her daughter's clandestine affair being discussed before the public. Now, all that was left was the sentencing. It was set for the following week. That would give the families of the victim time to make their statements.

After his outburst and guilty plea at the trial, he had been told about Marlo's identical twin. He had believed he was seeing Marlo's ghost but after learning about Kat, he felt that he had been made a fool of and asked his attorney if he couldn't do something.

His attorney shook his head and said, "No way, I'm through. Your brother spent a bundle of money on you, preparing a defense, but you threw it all away. Now, you can live with it. You said you were guilty, after all.

"Throughout the following week, Tish wrote and

rewrote what she was planning to say to the Judge before the sentencing. There was so much she wanted to express about her old friend. Nothing she wrote seemed adequate. And, there was the pain she herself had experienced. Joseph, Marlo's fiancé, was undecided about whether or not he should travel to the trial to make a statement. He had never seen Alex and really preferred to remember Marlo as she was with him, not with Alex. Finally, he decided not to come but sent a written statement which he asked be read:

"Marlo and I were very much in love and planned to share our lives together. This man took not only her life but our combined lives, our marriage, any children we might have had. He destroyed it all, brutally. I ask the court to impose the harshest sentence allowable under the law."

When Tish rose to speak, she felt herself starting to cry but managed to regain composure. She approached the bench and said, simply, "He really hurt me, Judge, when he beat me like he did. It's a miracle that I'm still alive. I wish you would lock him up forever, for the rest of his life, without parole."

Ralph and Gloria Scott stood together before the judge. Gloria sobbed softly while Ralph told of their sorrow at the loss of who they believed was their only child.

When the victim statements were over, it was Alex turn to speak.

He stated what his lawyer had encouraged him to say, "I'm sorry for what I did. I have changed while I have been in jail awaiting trial. I ask for mercy not only for my sake, but for my wife and children's sake." His wife's absence was noticeable.

The judge, however, responded without mercy. When the sentence was read, it was what all had asked for: life without the possibility of parole.

Alex hung his head as he was led away, casting one last furtive glance at Kat.

13

SUPREME COURT HEARS CASE

As spring came unleashing the traditional beauty of East Tennessee with the flowering redbuds blooming in profusion, followed by the dogwood trees revealing their special flowers next. The woods were dotted with the white splashes against the darkened winter wood, now quietly coming alive with a hint of early green showing here and there. Yards in neighborhoods showed off canopies of white spirea and azaleas soon after the flowering quince and buttercups came and went away, bitten by the usual late frosts.

The warming weather seemed to energize people causing them to act like children getting out of school for recess; they went outdoors to exercise and play. Seems like most had a favorite sport, whether it was golf, horseback riding, or hiking, whatever, these people greeted the season with great appreciation.

More than a year passed before the case was heard by the Supreme Court. People on both sides were growing impatient to know what they believed would be the final outcome.

Finally, on April 18, 1978, the case of TVA vs Hank Hill was argued before the U.S. Supreme Court. The young lawyers were greatly outnumbered by the gaggle of TVA attorneys. In spite of having their own experienced lawyers, TVA had Attorney General Griffin Bell argue their case. Hank Hill said he thought Bell looked silly dressed in his morning coat with tails. Plater, on the other hand was dressed in a normal suit, as most attorneys dressed for any court appearance. Plater argued for Hill who represented the river and all who wanted to save it. After the case was heard, more waiting had to be endured.

It was not until June 15, 1978, that the case was decided and announced. Hank Hill had won! It was a six to three ruling in favor of the snail darter and the river. The justices who sided with Plater and Hill were the following: John Paul Stevens, Warren Burger, Thurgood Marshall, Byron White, Potter Stewart, and W.J. Brennon Jr. Four of the six justices were appointed to the court by Republican presidents, Eisenhower, Nixon and Ford, while two were appointed by Democrat presidents, Kennedy and Johnson. Ironically, the three dissenters, William Rehnquist, Lewis F. Powell, Jr, and Harry Blackman, betrayed the environmental values of Nixon who had appointed them. It just confirmed the fact that presidents could not control what the justices decided once they were seated on the Court.

There was great jubilation throughout the valley and the entire nation as many people celebrated a case likened to the Biblical David and Goliath battle. Some faculty members at the University of Tennessee felt a little stupid knowing they had favored Plater's ouster from the institution. Others were secretly glad he wasn't around to compete for favoritism among the students. None of the other law professors had ever even argued a case before the Supreme Court, much less won one against the government itself. Kat filled her publication with photos of the excited resistors who loved the river. She put a photo of the river on the front page of the *Gazette*. It was, nevertheless, somewhat sobering to see the devastation of its banks, shorn as if with giant scissors, bare of vegetation. Gone were the beautiful, picturesque trees near Chota. Many people, believing the fight was finally over, looked forward to nature's healing, knowing that seedlings would spring forth and vegetation would once again cover the barren ground so cruelly pushed about by the giant machinery.

Senator Howard Baker and TVA, especially Wagner, were absolutely furious. They were literally outraged by the outcome. It had become a personal vendetta and Baker was determined not to be outdone. He conspired with Senator Culver and Congressman Robin Beard in the House to secure passage of an amendment to the Endangered Species Act which would set up a committee with the power to grant exceptions in some federal projects if the project was more valuable than the species endangered. Clearly, the amendment was meant for the Tellico Project. It passed. Many politicians preferred to have someone else, like those on the committee, make the decision and help them avoid possible political fall-out.

Meanwhile, some people were continuing to lobby members of Congress, both for and against saving the Little Tennessee River. Democrat Albert Gore, Jr. was elected to represent Tennessee's 4th District House of Representatives in 1977 after Joe L. Evins announced his retirement. Ironically, it was Evins who had defeated his father, Gore Sr. back in the 50's. While young Albert, still in his 20's, was campaigning, he seemed to care about the environment and the people of the state. Therefore, Hank Hill, the plaintiff in the Endangered Species case against TVA was very excited and hopeful that Gore would be on the side of the opponents and would try to help save the river. Hill continued to visit D.C. as often as possible trying to meet as many members of the House and Senate as he could, pleading his cause of trying to save the Little T. He had found a sympathetic ear in Congressman J. Murphy who represented a district in another state.

"Hank," Congressman Murphy said, "if you can get some of Tennessee's elected congressmen and senators, even just one, that would go a long way toward influencing other members of Congress. You know, most of us look to the people elected from whatever state is going to be impacted . . . you know, to determine whether to be for or against a project."

Hill was very optimistic about the prospects of getting support from at least one of Tennessee representative, Albert Gore Jr. He rode the elevator up to Gore's office and was welcomed by a smiling receptionist who ushered him into the inner office where the Congressman was waiting.

"He graciously thanked me for visiting him and said he was 100 percent for the snail darter and the river." Hill was elated. He walked back down to Congressman Murphy's office, not bothering to wait for the elevator, eager to share the good news because it was Murphy who had suggested that he needed someone from the Tennessee delegation to oppose the dam in order to gain the support of others, like himself, who were out-of-state representatives.

"I was dancing on air, really believing that Gore Jr. meant what he said about being against the dam, but, boy, was I ever in for a surprise."

When I returned to Murphy's office, his secretary took me inside and asked me to have a seat, gesturing to a chair in front of the Congressman's desk.

"He'll be right back" she said.

As I sat there waiting, the speaker phone came on and I heard it blaring away. It was Al Gore spewing forth a tirade of rhetoric saying that he was tired of the wackos, ecology freaks, crazy nuts, communists, trying to stop a much-needed project. He then admonished Murphy to stop sending people like me to see him. Needless to say, I was dumbfounded. Only moments earlier, Albert Gore Jr. had lied right to my face!"

Back in Tennessee, hope was diminished as the river people knew that the committee was merely a political tool set up by Baker and his associates. Because the committee had power over life and death, it was quickly nicknamed the God Committee. It was to be composed of the following: the Agricultural Secretary Bob Bergland, Army Secretary Clifford Alexander, Council of Economics Advisor Charles Schultz, Environmental Protection Agency Administrator Douglas Costle, and National Oceanic and Atmospheric head Richard Franch. Baker was quite pleased with himself. No one could question the ethics of such a high-brow group of the bureaucrats on the committee. Baker and his cronies felt extremely optimistic.

However, Baker and his crony-capitalist conspirators were in for another shock when on January 23, 1979, the God Committee reported their unanimous decision to deny the exemption.

A quote from Charles Schultz was straight to the point, " . . . *here is a project that is 95 percent complete, and if one takes just the cost of finishing it against the total benefits and does it properly, it doesn't pay, which says something about the original design!"*

Outraged that his clever plan had back-handed him politically, Baker once again began to search for yet a new plan to get his way. This time he conspired with Congressman John Duncan Sr. who represented the district where TVA's powerful central office was located and, also, the dam and project area. Naturally, other members of Congress would want to support him. Representatives tended to yield to those who supposedly represented the people of the area. And so, on June 18, in a late afternoon session of the House of Representatives, with many of the members absent, Congressman Duncan rose to make an amendment to exempt the Tellico Project from the Endangered Species Act. The amendment was not read and passed by a voice vote.

Baker was elated and came out to force the rider through the Senate. On his first try, on July 17, his attempt failed, 45 to 53 against. He again, was outraged and TVA was coming down hard on him, losing confidence in their special senator. He vowed to try again and used every trick in his political arsenal to change the minds of those who had voted against him. It took him about two months, but on September 11, he was ready to try again. This time, a weary group of senators voted a second time on his rider. The bill passed by only four votes.

Opponents in the valley were demoralized. They had come to believe the river would be saved in spite of the devastation and rape of the land around it. The hold-outs had come to believe their diligence and long suffering had been rewarded. Now, this new twist in the never-ending battle left them reeling with anger and sadness. Only the hope of a possible veto by President Jimmy Carter could save them now.

Major newspapers were quick to comment and papers with both liberal and conservative leanings tended to share the same sentiment.

Kat quoted from major newspapers published the following day, September 12, 1979:

The Christian Science Monitor wrote, "The TVA itself has called it a planning misjudgment which, if completed, might cost more jobs than it saves . . . The question is just what was 'won' when the Senate joined the

House in exempting the $115 million Tellico Dam, a boondoggle if ever there was one . . ."

The Washington Star, "Senator Baker, by combining pork barrel with presidential aspirations, may have chosen a precarious case to challenge the president . . ."

Sentinel Star, Orlando, Florida, stated, "When the U.S. Senate caved in this week to authorize completion of the Tellico Dam in Tennessee, its vote symbolized everything that is wrong with Congress."

Kat threw the paper she was reading across the room. "Now, they are against it when before, all they could write about was people vs a little fish! That's the problem with the media, always looking for something sensational, strange, whatever . . ."

On the days to follow, more and more newspapers continued to express similar thoughts.

On September 13, the *Portland Oregonian* wrote, "It may be easy for some to joke about the 'snail darter mentality,' that would permit the completion of a dam whose economic benefits will be less than the cost of finishing the nearly completed project. It is hard to find a worse case of misuse of public funds . . . The Tellico project followed skullduggery in the House."

On September 14, *The New York Times*, wrote, "If the Tennesseans prevail, they will have created a precedent for further efforts to exempt pork-barrel projects from all laws and rational review."

That same day, *the Boston Globe* published the following: "The approval of Tellico does not merely raise the somewhat rarified issue of endangered species, but casts in bold light the whole issue of congressional pork barrel legislation."

On the following Monday, September 17, *Chicago Tribune* wrote, "No one with a national perspective can congratulate Sen. Baker on his victory for the Tellico Dam. He should have conceded defeat long ago, to the finding that the dam is not worth having."

On Thursday, September 20, Kat found two more newspaper editorials.

The *Philadelphia Inquirer* had the following perspective: "That the dam itself is wasteful is beyond reasonable dispute . . . totally unjustified from a standpoint of economic benefits . . . it would kill far more than the snail darter, including a great deal of superb unspoiled countryside and valuable farmland for no useful purpose. Wiping away legal protection to push a pet project through is an unacceptably dangerous precedent."

The *Los Angeles Times,* "Tellico: A dam waste . . . The more persuasive reason for halting the project is that its potential economic benefits to the region are nil . . . Tellico has been a pork-barrel project from the very beginning."

Kat scattered the various newspapers over a big table in her office and remarked to Tish, "I sure hope Carter reads all of these editorials and vetoes the thing. My favorite quote is the one in the *Philadelphia Inquirer* because it talks about the land being lost. Most of the others just refer to the economics. Wonder why more people don't appreciate farmers?"

Tish shook her head, "I really don't know. They eat every day; you'd think they'd appreciate the fact that farmers are responsible for that. And, did you know that the average yield of corn per acre in the Little Tennessee valley is 55 bushels while the national average is only 23? This very year, the harvest on Rose Island was 60 bushels per acre! Imagine, covering up that kind of soil. "

Kat, half listening, continued poring over a stack of newspapers. "Here are a couple more editorials," Kat said. "This one is from *the Houston Post*," She opened the newspaper and began to read, "By a legislative rabbit-in-the-hat trick the House of Representatives has exempted the big, costly, impractical Tellico Dam in Tennessee of legal impediments. The move is in slick defiance of all the reasoned judgement . . ."

Kat folded the *Post* and picked up a copy of *Times* Magazine, and read from it, "Though Mayor Charles Hall of Tellico Plains, population 1,000, predicts the project will create 10,000 jobs over the next two decades, a new report by the Tennessee Valley Authority and the U.S. Department of Interior concludes that the river and the farm land untouched would have brought even more jobs . . . And TVA now admits it will not even provide the power for which it was built. Practicality lost to politics."

"Wow, "Tish said, "I'm so glad you have put all these quotes together. I wish more people could see how the whole nation sees this terrible tragedy that's been happening here for years now, driving people off their land, pushing the good dirt, digging up bones." She paused, then said, "No pun intended. I'm not talking about the Randy Travis song. I'm talking about them digging up the remains of all those Cherokee buried in the mounds along the river. It's terrible what landowners here have gone through, even though some of their greedy neighbors have turned against them, pushing for TVA all the way. I just hate greed. I truly believe it is the root of all evil."

"I know, but remember, Tish, what your father told you. Not everyone is as smart as you are. Some of the TVA supporters are just gullible. Because they think TVA has done some good things in the past, they want to believe them now. These people can't think for themselves. They've been told what to believe and they've bought into the propaganda." Kat replied.

"Oh, I know, but I still think there are more self-serving, greedy people than dumb gullible ones. All these planning groups have political appointees, most of whom are 'yes' people. You know, they just go along like mindless robots."

"Of course, that's why they were appointed in the first place. They've already been indoctrinated by TVA-controlled politicians, and there are many. TVA has the money and the votes. It's not just the employees but their families. Just think how many votes every TVA employee influences, their spouses, and their extended families all of whom want so-and-so to keep their job. It's like that with all these government agencies and even local boards and groups, they command big blocks of votes so they get what they want." Kat said, and then added, "It's the same all over. Special interest groups have found a way to circumvent the will of the people and most people don't even know it."

"I really respect the TVA employees who were against the taking of land. They were what you might say, between a rock and a hard place, choosing to work against their convictions or giving up their jobs. Some of them did walk away while others lobbied in secret against the dam, but to no avail." Tish said.

"I know. That's why I think the Scarecrow might actually be a TVA employee. Maybe that's why he has never been caught." Kat said.

Tish bit her lip because she almost forgot her promise and was about to let it slip that Julie believed it was her husband Jimmy who was the Scarecrow.

"Speaking of TVA employees, Vonore Mayor Fred "Fizz" Tallent told Fran Dorward that TVA had sixty-two thousand employees in the 60's and may still have that many on their payroll. That's a lot of votes! And multiply that number if you count family members who also consider paychecks when they vote." Kat said.

"You know, much of old Vonore was already destroyed when I got here, but Mayor Tallent paints a pretty picture of a busy little village that bustled before TVA started buying people out. He said Vonore had two general stores, two barbershops, three beauty shops, a drugstore, post office, a pulpwood yard, a sawmill, a hardware and feed store, mechanic shop, a restaurant, and gas stations., and lots of churches. He explained that people visited back and forth between the churches which were important for the social life of everyone and especially, the young people. They would have hayrides and wiener roasts, all chaperoned, of course, with church folks. "Kat repeated what she had been told.

"Yes, most of the people who lived in the valley were good, hard-working Christian people who lived by the Golden Rule. And, they believed if you treated people fairly and honestly, people would reciprocate and treat you the same, but that didn't happen here." Tish sighed.

"Mayor Tallent also told me that fish caught in the Little Tennessee River tasted better than fish caught in other places. Is that true?"

"Yes, it's true. In the spring when the fish are running, people catch a dozen varieties. They're better because of the clear, cold, clean water that is not contaminated like lakes and other rivers. We need to have a fish fry so you can see for yourself . . . before it's too late."

14
POLITICIANS SIGN DEATH WARRANT

No one knew for sure how long it would take the President to decide whether or not to sign the exemption into law. He could always veto it. After all, these were Republicans who had sneaked the bill through both the House and the Senate, and by a very narrow majority, only four votes in the Senate, so Carter could easily choose to veto the bill. Opponents hoped that a veto would happen. Quickly, they sent their letters begging, pleading, and doing whatever they could do to try to influence Carter.

On September 25, President Jimmy Carter signed the exemption into law. Big Democrat loyalist Mayor Charles Hall of Tellico Plains was pleased to report that Carter phoned him from Air Force One to congratulate him. It is believed that Hall was a significant contributor to the Carter campaign.

And, so it was that two Republicans, John Duncan Sr. and Howard Baker, and one Democrat, Jimmy

Carter, together signed the death warrant of the Little Tennessee River. The Republicans who had supported passage of Nixon's Endangered Species Act and fought to save the rich, historic valley and the river that flowed through it hung their heads in shame. Strangely, many Democrat zealots were able to forgive Carter for not vetoing the bill, blaming only the Republicans. Those who lost their homes and their way of life blamed both parties.

There was great disappointment in various places throughout the United States as some began to realize just how much power government and their agencies have over their lives.

On October 17, a long and scathing letter was published in *The Cherokee One Feather*, a North Carolina newspaper published by the Tribal Council of the Eastern Band of Cherokee. The letter listed in numerous columns detailed information about the economic and commonsense reasons why the Little Tennessee River and valley should be saved, and adds the following:

"The dam will violate many pieces of landmark legislation including the Endangered Species Act, the National Historic Preservation Act, the National Environmental Policy Act, the Rivers and Harbors Act, and the Executive Order on Floodplain Management. One wonders why we have any laws at all.

"Conservative James Buckley said last month: 'It is imprudent to allow an estimate of immediate worth, as perceived by men trained to think in terms of only near-term

goals, to be the basis for deciding whether a given species is to be preserved.'

"We challenge the Tennessee media to meet their responsibility in reporting this issue.

"Long live the Little T!"

The letter was signed Richard Wilkey, Chairman, Wildlife Committee, Sierra Club, Tennessee Chapter, and Randy Brown, President, Trout Unlimited, Appalachian Chapter.

15
CHEROKEES LAST STAND

As a last ditch effort, the Eastern Band of Cherokee filed a law suit to try to save their historic places, but held little hope that they would prevail. They organized a Camp-out to be held on October 19-20, 1979.

It was with great disappointment and anger that many of the long struggling valley opponents of the dam decided to go join the weekend campout at Chota in support of the Cherokee. They were joined by many others from outside the region as well who opposed killing the river. For some, it was a time to mourn and say goodbye.

As for political blame, the resentment was bipartisan. Baker, all puffed up from his treachery against President Richard Nixon now felt no loyalty for the popular environmental protection law championed by the former President. Baker acted extremely pompous and self-righteous while he was on television during the Watergate hearings, yet sunk to kill a river in near secrecy. Opponents of the dam, especially in Tennessee, would never forgive him for his betrayal of the landowners and the river nor would they forgive the actions of Congressman John Duncan Sr. who thereafter was rumored to be in the pocket of TVA. Of course, they didn't excuse Democrat President Jimmy Carter for signing the amendment which excluded the Tellico Dam from the Endangered Species Act.

It was a beautiful October weekend when people began to gather there at Chota. The event had been highly publicized and people traveled from many places to show their support of the Cherokees, of the landowners, and their genuine love and appreciation of the Little Tennessee River. Kat was going to camp out all weekend and cover the story in her paper. Julie, Jimmy, Tish, Neil, and numerous other local opponents were also planning to attend.

As one carload of Jensen Valley folks, including Tish and Neil, were driving up the road that led to the large flat field where the campers were gathering, Neil noticed some glints from shiny objects on the road.

"Stop!" he said rather loudly.

Jimmy braked suddenly, causing the passengers to pitch forward. Neil jumped out and picked up one of the nails which had been exposed by bright rays from the sun. Then they noticed an out of town car off the side of the road a little further up. It had sustained a flat tire.

"I don't suppose anyone has a broom!" Jimmy said.

"I've got a little whisk broom in here," Julie exclaimed. "It'll be better than nothing, don't you think?"

They began picking up the nails that they could see, Julie bent over and whisked where a number of the nails seemed to be scattered. Meanwhile, Neil walked to the automobile with the flat tire. The driver, alone in the car, was poking around the trunk looking for a spare. He looked up when Neil approached.

Neil could see that the stranded driver was a Native American. He stuck out his hand and introduced himself, "I'm Neil Darren and I believe you could use some help."

"I'm John Hair," the driver said in return. I flew into the Knoxville airport and rented this car so I don't have a clue if it has a jack, but I see a spare."

They changed the tire while the others continued the clean-up of nails, assisted now by others from cars lining up behind them.

"Can you believe this!" someone grumbled.

A uniformed officer approached them and warned them to be diligent, "There have been threats made by some of the local idiots, probably some of those Charles Hall/TVA worshippers, so be careful." The officer was an opponent of the project. "We did find a small amount of dynamite, but we think the place is safe if the thugs don't get in here. I'm here to see that the ones I know will stay the hell out, but there may be some I don't know."

"Thanks for the information," Kat said, waved and walked over to where Neil and John Hair were standing. She was impressed by the appearance of the handsome Cherokee standing before her, thinking that he could be a movie star with such a stunning appearance. Black hair, black, piercing eyes in a well-chiseled face, above a perfect body!

"Since I have always wanted to see the ancestral place of my ancestors, I figured I needed to come see it now before it's too late." Looking at the nails in the road, he shook his head and said, "I knew the dam was controversial, but I never thought there would be objections to us Cherokees having a camp-out. Although it's a protest, no one expects us to be able to stop the thing. I thought the Indian wars were over," he said laughing.

Kat proceeded to talk to him and asked if she could interview him for her paper. He agreed and said he would be glad to talk to her after he set up his tent and got settled. He said he needed to talk to a few of the other Cherokees he had promised to see when he arrived.

Neil and Jimmy put up one large tent flanked by some smaller ones. Thankfully, the weather forecast promised a dry weekend and hoped Mother Nature would keep the promise. The diverse crowd mingled. In addition to the landowners and opponents who lived in the area, fisherman and others who enjoyed the Little T had come, some from great distances, as had history buffs, environmentalists, and naturalists of all kinds. Most came to support the Cherokee who had traveled from their reservation in North Carolina to protest and make a last ditch effort to stop the flooding of their remaining burial grounds and their historical capitol, Chota.

Kat was spellbound by it all. So intense was she to give an accurate portrayal of the event, she moved from one little cluster of people to another asking questions and taking notes. As the sun set, reflected light on the moving waters of the Little Tennessee looked like diamonds dancing across the surface. Campfires burned long into the night and people sat around them, long after their hotdogs were roasted and eaten. Finally a hush fell over the campground as people were stilled by their need of sleep. Some crawled into their tents while others slept in bedrolls under the stars. Still others climbed into the beds of pick-up trucks.

The next day, Kat woke early and saw other early risers including John Hair. She decided he would be the primary subject of a story. He had come all the way from Oklahoma where his great-grandparents had been forced to go on the Trail of Tears so many years before. A Tennessean, President Andrew Jackson, had caused that. Now, these current Tennesseans had gone so far as to dig up the bones of his earlier ancestors. It was difficult to comprehend how they could just pile them into boxes and store them in a basement at the University of Tennessee. It seems that people respect graves only as long as immediate survivors are around, then no one cares. She sighed and continued listening.

"The Cherokees used to refer to the river as 'Strong Waters'" one older Cherokee explained.

Kat agreed, these waters were strong, not only in their movement, but also in the intense feeling this river evoked. Perhaps there was truly something spiritual here. For some reason, she was moved and knew her instincts were stronger; she realized that a great travesty was going to soon take place. It must have been Déjà vu because she felt like she had been in this place before.

Kat went straight home following the weekend event and wrote the following story which was printed in the next issue of the *Valley Gazette:*

> *When My Eyes Close Forever,*
> *Don't Forget My Bones*

John Hair, a full-blooded Cherokee whose ancestors survived the Trail of Tears from Tennessee to Oklahoma 141 years ago, had heard much about his roots in Chota on the banks of the Little Tennessee River, but had never seen it for himself.

A striking well-dressed man who wore not symbols but the pride of his race as seen in his eyes, the piercing black gaze of one who appears to see more than the horizon. John Hair arrived at Knoxville's airport in the early afternoon Saturday, October 20, 1979, to visit the ancient burial grounds of his ancestors. He had always planned to see the place as dear to the hearts of the Cherokee as Jerusalem is to Christians and Jews. Chota wasn't just a burial ground; it had been the capitol of the Cherokee nation, the place where the legendary Sequoyah, the inventor of the Cherokee alphabet was born.

He knew he could no longer delay seeing Chota, for should the government fail to honor the laws designed to protect Indian rights, the valley and the river would soon be lost to the dead waters of yet another lake. And, he certainly was not optimistic about the government promises to the Cherokee because history had shown him that those promises were pretty much always broken. He made his living as an airline pilot and had been able to travel the world, certainly not bound to staying on a reservation; nevertheless, he had never stopped valuing his heritage.

As Vice-Chief of the Keetoowah Band of Cherokee in Tahlequah, Oklahoma, John Hair was not surprised by the actions of congress in ignoring the Indian feelings in relation to the Tellico decision. He was, however, surprised by the attitude of some local people. At the airport, he rented a car and drove to Monroe County. Stopping along the way, he was surprised that no one he encountered could or would give him directions to Chota, site of the well-publicized camp-in. If the people had never seen Chota, he wondered, why were they so anxious to flood it? If they had seen it, why did they wish to deny him an opportunity to see it? At 5 p.m., John Hair finally discovered the location, guided mainly by the homing instinct and remembered directions from other Cherokees.

When he first saw Chota, the spirit of its beauty, the power of its landscape, his heart began to beat faster and he knew he was there. It was as he had visualized it. John Hair, used few words to speak of his feelings, but as he stood and looked beyond, from the sky to the mountains, the river and the autumn meadows, his expression was a statement. He quoted one of his old uncles, 'When my eyes close forever, don't forget my bones.'

John Hair made no speeches at the camp but others spoke and explained some of the differences between the beliefs of Native Americans and those of the white people.

"The single most significant difference," Lloyd Sequoyah said, "is his relationship to his environment. The whites believe they have dominion over all things while the Indian does not. We believes all things in nature are important, the rocks, the trees, animals, all things. Our belief in the Great Spirit is symbolized by a trinity of nature, the Father Sun, the Mother Earth, and Grandmother Moon." After a pause, he continued, "as our history relates, because of the Cherokees appreciation of all creations, he welcomed as brothers the paler people who came from across the sea. Yet we were called savage and they, civilized." The old fellow with the European first name and the Cherokee surname shook his head slowly.

An elderly woman Ollie Otter was flanked by two Cherokee youngsters who seemed to be her helpers. They were silent with somber expressions which revealed nothing. It was the hope of the elder tribe members that the young people would remember the place.

All of the opponents of the project who were gathered there on the site of the ancient village, the Cherokees, farmers, bus drivers, mail carriers, fisherman, historians, the mixed group of rank and file citizens, all seemed to be comforted by being among the hundreds of like-minded people. And, as campfires burned brightly into the night and the musical group called Crazy Creek from a settlement near Citico played the foot-stomping bluegrass music of the country south, when the fiddle whined and the banjo gave rhythm to their feelings, when an old felt hat with a feather sticking from it, labeled the Cherokee Lawsuit Hat was placed on a stand, Kat not only contributed money but was pleased to see, while the lyrics of an old song about "the fox on the run" was sung, others also placed money into the hat.

Following the camp-out, much of the national media focused on the vile behavior of those who had placed dynamite about the site and threw nails onto the road. They also showed some of the tacky, ignorant signs made by some of the pro-dam people in addition to professionally designed ones by TVA enthusiasts.

What could have been a wonderful view of the good people of the region was not seen; rather it was the bad and ugly. Kat, of course, published a different perspective of the event, but her readers were far fewer in number than the millions exposed via the national media. It was like preaching to the choir, she thought. I wish the national media would have come here sooner and dug deeper into the issues. Most of them didn't speak out until after the exemption was passed, then, they heaped on the criticism. They seem more interested in showing controversy than publishing facts.

After her story of the Camp-out was published, she began to get subscriptions from Cherokees with addresses all over the country. She got letters from a group in Alabama as well as from Oklahoma and North Carolina. But, since the courts had refused to act on the Cherokee lawsuit and had denied their request to halt the project to preserve their historical sites, Kat had become dismal, questioning whether or not she should keep publishing her little paper. She was moved by the letters from the Cherokees who had responded not only to her coverage of the Camp-out weekend, but also, letters to other publications which indicated widespread disappointment.

In response to the article "When My Eyes Close Forever, Don't Forget My Bones," John Hair wrote the following letter:

"Thank you so very much for reaffirming my faith in all peoples.

"Your article was beautiful and naturally I will treasure it.

"I went to Cherokee, N.C. for two days – what beautiful country, the Little T, the valleys, the mountains, the people, most of those I met.

"The TSA LA GI YA Club of Tulsa is sending for some of your publication of which a number are spoken for by me.

"If anything of interest develops in your area, I would appreciate hearing from you. I would be honored if you would stay in touch."

> John Hair, Assistant Chief,
> United Keetoowah Band of Cherokee,
> Oklahoma

The Eastern Band of Cherokee wasted no time in seeking an injunction after September 25, the day that President Jimmy Carter signed the bill and failed to veto the exemption which had been orchestrated by Baker and Duncan. However, the Cherokee Nation of Oklahoma failed to join the lawsuit. This decision was not popular with all of those who were members of the

Oklahoma tribe. There was a flurry of letters to the editors of Cherokee newspapers. One letter published at Tahlequah, Oklahoma, in *The Cherokee Advocate* had much to say about how that paper had covered the Tellico Dam controversy:

> *"I believe your paper has been remiss in not providing an adequate coverage of the issue and by not keeping your readers informed of the continuing developments."*
>
> *"The bill allowing completion of the dam passed the U.S. Senate by only a few votes and could have been vetoed by President Carter. If people of Cherokee ancestry throughout the country had been aroused and kept informed, some of those who voted for the bill might have been persuaded not to have done so. I know I was caught unaware, having thought the matter settled by the courts."*
>
> *In reference to the villages destined to be underwater, Corbett writes:*
>
> *"The sacred peace towns were the places of the eternal fire which burns invisibly inside the townhouse mounds. They were cities of refuge where no blood could be shed since the ground they stood on was holy. Of these towns, Great Echota was recognized as being the most ancient and sacred. Its loss is for the Cherokee people what the destruction of the Wailing Wall in Jerusalem would be for the Jewish people."*
>
> *The letter was signed, T.L. Corbett, Las Cruces, N.M.*

16
LAST ONES OUT

TVA was to waste no time now in preparing for the execution of the river since the courts had failed to give a reprieve through the Cherokee lawsuit. Tom Miller was given 15 days to move the house he had bought and all his belongings. On November 9, eviction notices were hand-delivered to the remaining hold-outs. If they were not out by Nov. 13, they would be forced out by federal marshals.

Since Tom Miller was not a land owner, few members of the press were aware of his plight.

"You'd be surprised at how fast 15 days can go when you're holding down a job and trying to move at the same time." Miller said. He explained how he had arranged for a contractor to move the house. Meanwhile, he, with the help of his family members, began packing. They asked TVA for a little more time because the contractor explained that weather had delayed his ability to move the house. Another family had been given a few extra days to move their belongings, but not Miller. It was in the black of night when TVA and federal marshals blocked the road to his home. A little girl in the family asked permission to get her playhouse out of the yard. The request was denied. A freezer was moved from the house. Within hours TVA had bulldozed the playhouse along with the large brick home. A child cried. A man was hand-cuffed and taken away.

Later, when Miller went back to the scene and recovered the freezer which was left intact, he opened it and discovered that the food was gone. It had contained the efforts of a summer. Tom's mother had filled it with the harvest of her labor. "It's not the cost of it in money," Tom said. "It's the principle. That food can't be replaced. It hurts us when people tell us we had years to move. We didn't know what the outcome of the lawsuit would be. Why couldn't TVA have given us a few more days . . . we weren't refusing to move."

It was not a pretty day, but it was not expected to be, even if the sun could have been seen through the dark and brooding clouds. There was stillness in the air and a sense of foreboding on that November day of 1979 when the last three of the hundreds of families were going to be evicted from their homes by federal marshals. One of the three was headed by a widow who had lost her husband during the struggle to save their farm and home. One was family of six, and the last was a bachelor who lived alone.

The first home to be visited by the federal marshals that day belonged to the Ritchey family; Ben and Jean and their four children. Their youngest was still in school but the two older daughters were grown and had become teachers. Their son was farming alongside his parents. All helped work the farm as was typical of family farms and it was income from their farm that sustained them. Knowing that the fight was lost and learning approximately when their home was going to be demolished, they had rushed to find a place for their cattle, and other livestock. They also had to move a barn full of tobacco, which had been hung to dry and not yet graded for sale. In addition, there was all the farm machinery and household furniture that had to be moved.

The haste seemed so unnecessary since their farm was not going to be underwater, but TVA was chomping at the bit to get rid of these embarrassing hold-out families. Wagner is said to have resented them for defying him, but had left the actual evictions up to his replacement. TVA's new Chairman David Freeman is on record as having resented Wagner for leaving the dirty work of evictions up to him, years after their properties were condemned. The Ritchey home as well as the property of the other two hold-outs was above the water line but within the taking line, a fact that few could explain away. It was the taking of one's land to resell to another, pure and simple.

The media from far and wide, local and national, had descended on the area once the fight was lost and Carter failed to veto the exemption.

"Too bad they couldn't have paid attention early on," Tish said, watching as more news crews gathered in front of the Ritchey home, waiting to watch the bulldozers push down the home and barns. While Tish and Kat were standing with the other onlookers, a middle-aged man dressed in khaki fatigues and a jacket strolled up with Alfred Davis, president of the Landowners Association. As Alfred moved among those gathered to watch, he was given nods and thanks by many who admired how hard he had tried to save the land. They knew that his forefathers were some of the first to settle in the valley.

"Kat, I want you to meet Al Wasserman of CBS," Alfred said. Kat shook the man's hand while Alfred continued, "He wanted to meet you because of the letter you wrote to the *Knoxville Journal*. He read it and came down here on account of what you said."

Wasserman nodded and said, "That was some letter. We had planned to do a feature on 60 Minutes but TVA is moving so fast now, guess we'll have to put it on the news."

Since journalism was her profession, Kat was greatly impressed that such a renowned national news team had come to cover the evictions of the last condemned landowners. She managed a stuttered thank you to Wasserman and listened to Davis.

"Since they have blocked access to the McCall home, I'm going to have to show these fellows how to sneak in another way so they can get photos. Do you all want to come?"

There was a chorus of "Yes" as all, including David Smiley, a photographer taking photos for Kat, answered.

"I hate to leave before they evict Jean Ritchey," Tish said, "but there is sure to be coverage of her leaving because this road is not blocked and neither is Beryl's. Guess TVA is mostly concerned about the image of an elderly woman being carted away. Guess they aren't too concerned about Ben and feisty Jean and stoic Beryl being chased away. This is the second time for Jean. When she was 20-years old, she and her family were evicted by TVA by eminent domain for the Watts Bar Dam."

"I hadn't heard that. Were there others?" Kat asked.

"Oh yes, several of the other families. I know the Graham family was one. I thought I told you about them. Right now, I can't remember who else."

"Well, we'd better go now because we'll have to walk in and it won't be an easy walk," Alfred interjected.

The little group left hurriedly. None of them knew where or how Alfred planned to get them to where they could see the McCall's place, but they trusted him.

While they were following Alfred, Kat asked Tish again if there were others who had faced evictions for earlier dams.

"Oh, yes. You have to remember, this is the 29th dam TVA has built and it was always the farmers who got evicted. I can't remember all of the families out of so many who have been evicted for this one, but a number of them previously suffered at the hands of TVA for the creation of other dams and lakes. As I said, when Jean Ritchey was young, her family was pushed out for the Watts Bar Dam, and the Graham family was evicted earlier for the Douglas Dam. And, believe it or not, poor old Myrtle Graham, Bill's widow who relocated in Loudon after TVA evicted them this time for the Tellico project, again lost land under eminent domain for a road! But the road didn't take her house and it was the State, not TVA that took it, so she got to keep on living there, right by the road."

Alfred slowed and stopped. They parked along a dirt road which was lined by heavy foliage and trees along an old fence row. They got out of their vehicles, closing the doors quietly, and whispering because they did not want to be escorted off of what was now TVA land. They walked briskly across one field through tall, dead grasses and came to a wooded area which contained brambles and bushes of various varieties. The limbs were low and heavy and provided a good blind, but made walking difficult. Bending over, they twisted and ducked as they moved closer until they could see from a distance the front porch of the McCall home beyond an open expanse.

"This is about as far as we can go without being seen," Alfred said.

The CBS crew sat down on the ground, cautioning everyone to be quiet. They began assembling their equipment which included the longest camera lenses Tish had ever seen. Next, the crew began crawling through the brush to get as close as they could without being seen. The others moved down the tree line about fifty yards away from the CBS crew, to access a different point of view, still within the canopy of overgrown brush. As they moved closer, they lay down on their stomachs and inched forward, very slowly so as not to attract any attention. It did not appear than anyone was looking their way but they did not want to take any chances. There they waited, almost afraid to whisper.

Finally, Tish whispered to Kat, "I sure hope I don't have to go to the bathroom."

Kat stifled a laugh, "Don't get me tickled."

"Shoosh!" someone admonished softly.

They were quiet. Even the woods were unusually silent, with no birds chirping or singing, not even the whirring sound of insects could be heard. They waited and watched. Kat had her camera ready, but her zoom was not nearly as powerful as those being used by the CBS crew.

Because TVA was worried about its own public image from the ouster of 85-year old Nellie McCall from her 90-acre Greenback farm, they had managed to have law enforcement officers block the access road at a great distance from her home, believing they could prevent reporters from taking photographs. But word had been leaked, so some reporters had spent the night in the McCall's living room where nothing had been removed. In fact, all of the furniture in the rather spacious farmhouse was still in its place, where it had been positioned years ago. When questioned about why she had left the furniture in place, Mrs. McCall replied, "TVA told me they would move everything for me. They know I don't have anybody, just one grown daughter, and we couldn't move all this stuff. And, of course, they know I wouldn't need it moved if it weren't for them stealing my land. Tears began to flow as they had on and off since Carter failed to veto the sneaky amendment put forth by Congressman John Duncan Sr. and Senator Baker, currently two of the most despised Republicans on the face of the earth, at least among farmers and environmentalists throughout the country. And, it wasn't just in Tennessee. All over the country, newspapers had plenty to say in the excerpts Kat had published in her little *Valley Gazette.*

It was not a long wait before the federal marshals arrived in their black automobiles. It seemed fitting that they were dressed in black suits. Several climbed the steps to the front door and knocked. As the door opened, they were surprised by the flashes from cameras as they entered the home. They had been assured of privacy while they did their dirty work, as they themselves described their task.

"Who are you people?" the chief marshal asked.

"Friends." Someone answered.

The marshal could see media insignia on the hats and jackets and even the cameras of some of the reporters. "Out," he shouted and waved his arm. I am here to talk to Mrs. McCall and I don't need an audience."

As the other marshals flanking him began to move towards the numerous people in the room, they began to exit. When the marshal was left with Nellie, he told her, "You know why we are here. I don't want to have to carry you or arrest you or make you into a felon, so I suggest you come with me. "

An exhausted Nellie simply nodded her head and

began to walk out with the marshal's hand on her elbow, ushering her out the door. The frail elderly lady walked bravely as tears glistened on her cheeks.

Meanwhile, in the woods, CBS filmed the stoic little lady as she emerged from her front door and was escorted into one of the big black marshal vehicles. And shortly after, they heard the unmistakable sound of a news helicopter which was also filming the event.

After Mrs. McCall was whisked away, the little throng of media in the woods was silent for a moment, having witnessed a very sad event in the life of an elderly lady. She was barely out of the driveway, when the heavy equipment operators went to work, devastating the home. TVA's promise to save her furniture was just another one of their many lies. The CBS crew continued to film, but Kat and Tish and their little ground left to go to the home of Beryl Moser, who was going to be the last one out.

They drove from the Greenback property to Vonore. Beryl's home and outbuildings were situated on five acres very near downtown Vonore, a community that had already been devastated by the taking line and lost roads. In the past, people who lived in Vonore were able to travel about a dozen miles along a winding road to trade in Loudon as they often chose to do. Before the dam, Loudon had numerous clothing stores, numerous grocery stores, car dealerships, and, of course, farm equipment dealers. The town also had what used to be called dime stores. Now, that road has been cut off because there is going to be a lake covering much of it, so trade in Loudon would not be feasible.

Vonore is losing its high school because there would not be enough students left in the area to justify a high school. Those students remaining will have to be bused all the way to Madisonville.

Many people had gathered in front of the Moser homeplace where Beryl continued to live. His two sisters were married with homes of their own but they continued to dote on their one brother who had sacrificed so much for his family. A boy of 12 when their father had died, he had worked and sacrificed for them all, becoming a man when he was still just a boy. Then barely of age, drafted into the army at a time when his mother was still alive and partly dependent on him. Since returning from Korea, he had worked at the Ford Motor Company and now was a mail carrier in Blount County. He had been fighting for the river and his home for a very long time, having been one of those who had attended the first Save the Little T organization back in the 60's. He was to be one of the first to fight and the absolute last one out.

Just as they had done in the McCall home, numerous members of the media had spent the night in his living room, not knowing whether or not they would be permitted to be inside today. Kat and her group, however, walked straight up to his porch without incident as spectators moved aside and let them pass. Most of the people gathered were friends and knew that Kat was sympathetic to their cause.

Once inside, Kat could see that Beryl was suffering emotional pain. His expression was grave, facial muscles taut, as he answered questions from the various reporters. He had relayed much information over the years, having traveled to D.C. 14 times, arguing for the river, against TVA. Kat could tell that Beryl was lost in his own private thoughts, even as he recited answers to members of the press. She wondered if he would physically attack the federal marshals when they came.

About that time, they arrived. There were 15 of them. Perhaps they feared there would be trouble. They repeated what they had done at the McCall place. The lead marshal going up the front porch steps first. Beryl met him at his front door. Photographers sprang to action. David Smiley, taller than any of the others, was right in the marshal's face. He captured a great close-up of the marshal's face. Other photographers pushed and shoved to get Smiley out of the way. He stood his ground.

The marshal told Beryl that he could avoid being labeled a felon if he walked out with him. Otherwise, he told him he would be fired from the U.S. Post Office if he were arrested and charged with a felony. Beryl, of course, knew all that and what he had to do. His anger was more towards TVA than the marshal. The marshals escorted Beryl away. His sisters cried as they watched him leave.

Beryl asked the marshal if he would be allowed to come back and watch as his homeplace was destroyed. He was worried about his dogs which had been placed in his dog lot below the house. The marshal assured him that his dogs would be all right and that he would be able to return later in the day and could watch if he wanted to. He was then escorted to one of his sister's homes.

As soon as Beryl was out of site, some of the marshals removed his hunting dogs from their lot and placed them in a vehicle used by the Animal Control officer who took them away. The dogs had no idea what was happening and looked bewildered. They were driven to what was then called the Pound in Loudon. Shortly after, the heavy machinery operators went to work and proceeded to demolish the old well-built home along with the dog house and other outbuildings. Soon, it was pushed into a pile of rubble.

When Beryl returned to the site, that is all he could see, a big heap of rubble. He didn't know where his dogs were. Later that day, the phone rang in his sister's home. It was from the Loudon County Animal Shelter in Loudon where his dogs had been taken. They wanted him to come and get them.

Beryl said, "You bring them back. You took them, I didn't take them, so you better bring them back." And, so, later that day, the dogs were returned to Beryl. Emotionally shattered but still brave and stoic, Beryl and his pets sat together and were comforted by each other, the dogs resting their heads on his knee as he gently stroked their heads

And, so it had ended, with the last man out. On November 29, 1979, TVA closes the gates and begins impounding the Little T. While TVA leaders and proponents of the project celebrated, a heavy gloom hung over the valley. Large raindrops, like tears fell, inexplicably. Many of the displaced continued to pray, trying to find some solace for their plight, some trying to forgive those who had done them harm, still others asking for help dealing with the hatred and bitterness that crippled them and robbed them of their former happy lives.

A major story in the December issue of Oklahoma's *Cherokee Advocate* had a bitter heading: "Tellico Dam Gates Fall, River Begins to Rise."

The story that followed gave a brief listing of the last failed attempts to stop the project and continued, "And so, just before noon on November 29, the waters of the Little Tennessee River began to back up against the steel gates dropped into place at the Tellico Dam in Tennessee." It   quoted the bitter reaction to the decision to complete the project as expressed by Eastern Band Chief John A. Crowe who said, "I cannot find words strong enough to convey my contempt for the lack of honor to be found among TVA and federal officials."

*"I cannot find words strong
enough to convey my contempt for
the lack of honor to be found among
TVA and federal officials"
Chief John A. Crowe
Eastern Band of Cherokee*

17
THE AFTERMATH

As the days passed and the lake began to fill, some die-hard river enthusiasts took their boats to spend time in the last of the river while it continued to flow. Jimmy Smith was one of them. It was late in the afternoon when he returned home after having been out in his boat, looking at the valley slowly vanishing around him. Jimmy was a big man, burly in appearance, who seemed to be as stoic as any man could be. But, he sank wearily into his favorite chair, put his face in his hands and wept. Julie went to him and sat on the arm of the chair, rubbing his back and trying to comfort him.

Looking up at her he said, "Oh, Julie, the fish and even the snakes seem confused. I've never seen anything like it. God's creatures know what's normal and what's not. I declare, I hate TVA with every bone in my being. This is against nature, against what's supposed to be."

"I know, Jimmy, I hate it too. If it weren't for Ma

and Pa getting older, I'd be for picking up and moving as far away from here as I could go, somewhere out of TVA's reach. They are just like the gestapo, marching in here and taking over, pushing everyone around."

Days moved into weeks with the lake forming from the struggling, dying river. Finally, it covered all that it was designed to cover. Many people were surprised at the numerous bulldozed sites of former homes that remained above water. Curious, many residents drove around the area, looking at the changes. It was one such cloudy afternoon when Linda Hudson and a friend drove out from Loudon towards Monroe County. They were passing where the Ritchey home used to stand.

"Why, I thought Jean Ritchey didn't know what she was talking about when she said they were going to take her house even though it wouldn't be under the water." Mabel Swan said, "Well, I'll be, she was right! Right there," Mabel pointed, "is where her house sat. I heard on television that the lake was full now, so why'd they take her house?"

"Greed." Linda Hudson said. "Don't you remember when former Judge Simpson said it was a land-grab, a make-work project for TVA, and a sell-out of the farmers. "

"Yes, but *the Knoxville News-Sentinel* and the *Tri-County Observer* said the dam was going to be a bring factories to provide jobs."

"That's what TVA told them and that newspaper was, at least in the beginning, all pro-TVA. On the other hand, the *Knoxville Journal* printed both sides of the issue, not just what TVA says. As a result, some TVA backers tried to hurt the *Journal.* As for the local *Observer,* it's an independent paper and its owner makes his living selling ads. His biggest backer is Charles Hall of Tellico Plains whose telephone company will have to hang lots of new wire with all the changes the lake has made. I heard he got a million dollar rural development grant; that's like getting a loan that doesn't have to be repaid. "

"I heard Hall was the only local person who personally came to the site to watch TVA close the gates on the dam. You reckon that's true?"

"I don't know, but I wouldn't be surprised. " Linda said. She continued to drive until the pavement went into the lake. Barriers and signs had been erected to warn motorists. Still, in spite of the warnings and on-going publicity about the dam, one fatality had already occurred when a teenager drove over a bridge straight into the rising water.

The people who had fought so hard to save the Little T and the rich, productive bottom land that lay beside it, had grown quiet these days, grieving , mostly with thoughts turned inward, some growing more bitter as the days continued to pass; others trying to muster some hope for a future they had tried so hard to avoid, having to start over in a different place, a different way of life.

Tish had not been able to put the loss of the valley behind her. She had done only what she had to do and spent the rest of her time watching television or trying to escape in books because reading was one of her favorite past times.

January 20, 1980, was a cold day in January when she picked up the *Knoxville News-Sentinel* which Neil had tossed to her on his way back from the barn. She poured herself a fresh cup of coffee and sat down at the kitchen table and began reading letters to the editor. Many letters pertaining to the eviction of landowners had been written in the weeks since that fateful day.

Ironically, TVA Chairman David Freeman had written a letter less than two months from the time the gates to the dam were closed and the farmland flooded. The letter was written in response and in apparent agreement with the message penned by popular journalist Carson Brewer in his Sunday column "Loss of Prime Farmland Causes Widespread Concern for Future."

Freeman wrote: *"Carson and other thoughtful people have reminded us that every year we have been losing more of this country's most productive farmland to subdivisions, highways, dams, and industrial and commercial developments. Our people can't have jobs without economic growth, but over the long haul we will lose America's agricultural abundance if we continue to lose farmland."*

Freeman's letter continued:

"By the year 2000 this can be one of the toughest issues the country faces. We could start now to head off that crisis from unplanned development, but as yet we have no workable way to meet this problem. Today the confrontation between the farmer and the developer is

almost always an unequal contest, as Carson's column points out.

"The farmers usually lose – often willingly – because the people who have more intensive land uses in mind can call up more money and more aggressive arguments to back up their projects. There must be a better way to make these decisions, one that doesn't always sacrifice the long-term need for prime farmland to today's pressures for development.

"Many of us have seen what has happened to land around Knoxville in the last 25 years, and many of your readers must have some of the same worries about the loss of farmland. If people have ideas about practical approaches to help change this trend, we would like to see them."

Freeman concludes the letter with the address of TVA's office and encourages people to call the TVA Citizen Action Line. The letter is then signed, S. David Freeman.

Tish scoffed as she read the letter out loud to Neil as he was finishing his breakfast.

"Is he trying to make a joke or what! They just took 40,000 acres away from the farmers."

"Remember, Tish, it wasn't Freeman who caused it. Some of folks in the landowners association believe if Wagner had retired sooner, Freeman would have been able to get the alternate plan adopted. You know – farmers were going to make parcels available for industry if they could keep the rest. And, the plan also included methods for increasing tourism to all the historical sites. That plan would have provided a real economic impact." Neil rose, carried his plate to the sink, then carried the coffee pot to the table and poured both of them refills. Tish continued to stare at the newspaper as she listened to what Neil had to say.

"They think, I suppose without proof, that the politicians pushed for TVA's first plan to satisfy their greedy land-grabbing constituents. And, it is definitely true that some people will get rich from the farmer's land that our own government stole. There was that alternate plan that could have been accepted."

"I know what you're saying, Neil, I blame others more than I blame Freeman, but right now, I hate them all. It is so unfair!"

"Hate will hurt you, not them, Tish, but I *hate* for you to be so upset."

"I can't help it and I didn't even own any of the land that was flooded. Just imagine how those people feel who lost their ancestral home places. I would be heart-sick if they took our land, so I guess that's why I have so much empathy for them. But all of us lost the river and the valley."

"Let's go saddle a couple of horses," Neil said, grabbing Tish's hands and pulling her up from the chair. "You always feel better on a horse. It's your best therapy."

Looking down at herself, still dressed in flannel pajamas and wearing an old robe, Tish said, "Okay, but don't you think I ought to wear something else?"

Neil grinned at her, "Yes, you might spook the horses if you go to the barn dressed like that."

She smiled in spite of her gloomy mood, and rushed to the bedroom to pull on jeans and a heavy sweater. "How cold is it?"

"Cold." Neil said, "Remember, it's January. It might be too cold for us to ride, but we'll decide when we get to the barn . . . okay?"

The letter left former landowners scratching their heads, considering the fact that TVA had recently taken 40,000 acres out of production.

Neil, Tish, Julie, Jimmy and Kat found themselves spending more time together. They seemed to be comforted by the horses. Although Jimmy had never ridden near as much as the others, he, too, was becoming involved, even had Neil and Pa helping him search for a horse to buy.

"You can always ride one of ours," Neil told him, "you don't have to buy one."

"I know," Jimmy said, "but I want one of my own. I have to have something to take my mind off fishing." He missed fishing the Little T, something he had done since childhood.

"You not interested in fishing their new lake?"

"No. Even though it hasn't gotten polluted yet, like their other lakes, I can't enjoy fishing over all those fields they covered up. It's just too depressing."

One evening, Jimmy and Julie took the last river-caught fish out of their freezer and had a fish fry so that Kat could be certain to taste the best nature had to offer. Kat brought Roger Kinealy along. Apparently, Roger was changing his ways because Kat was the only woman he was seeing these days. Charles Thompson and his wife Paula were also invited. Charley had previously worked for former Senator Bill Brock who had opposed the Tellico Dam. In that capacity, he had helped Alfred Davis get paid for the rail fence TVA personnel had taken from his property. It was the principal of the thing.

It was a night of mixed emotions. They all found themselves more politically aware of the dangers government could impose on individuals. They found that humor helped them cope even while they were having serious discussions about the Bill of Rights and the U.S. Constitution.

Joking, Neil said, "You have a right to pursue happiness if you don't plan on farming."

Jimmy said, "You have a right to pursue happiness if you don't want to fish or float a river."

Tish added, "You have a right to own land if TVA doesn't want it."

On and on they would go, amid sarcastic laughter, each trying to come up with a different pursuit of happiness thwarted by TVA and politicians.

Together, they vowed to make sure that young people would know what had happened here.

18
REALITY BEGINS TO DAWN

As many months passed, and no new factories had shown any interest in locating along the lake, the citizens who remained in the area found a new pastime, heckling Charles Hall.

"Where are those jobs now, Hall?" Beryl Moser and others would say. "When are they going to start building all those factories?"

Hall would try not to show his resentment, but he had never shown any sympathy for the folks who disagreed with him. He would mumble something or ignore those who taunted him and focus on his band of followers. And, he certainly had followers including the ner-do-wells who were jealous and resentful of people who had something of value, like land and businesses along the river; also, the just plain greedy souls who saw a path for personal profit.

Most residents, however, might have simply been gullible, as Kat suggested, and believed the promises and pipe dreams that TVA had spun about the riches to come.

If TVA believed the controversy would finally go away after the gates were closed and the valley flooded, they were wrong. Not only did stories continue to be printed in area newspapers and in the Cherokee nations, both in North Carolina and in Oklahoma, national publications continued to write about the issues. For example, in his famous column, "Aboard at Home:"

> *Pulitzer prize winning writer Anthony Lewis stated, "It is only one dam, in a place unknown to most Americans, a parochial question, one might think. But it is not. The Tellico Dam is an extreme example of a widespread phenomenon in this country; the destruction of the land of the people who have worked it. What makes Tellico extreme is the way the thing was done. Logic, law and economics were overwhelming against it, but the facts availed nothing against the guile of cynical politicians."*

In the January, 1980 column titled "Ultimate Damage" distributed by *The New York Times* News Service, Lewis also referred to an article by another acclaimed writer, Peter Matthiessen, winner of the National Book Award among other awards. According to Lewis, the article which appeared in the New York Review of Books refuted in devastating detail every single argument that TVA had made.

"According to TVA itself, the annual cost of maintaining the dam will be greater than its income. The 'benefits' from the new lake will be nearly $1 million a year less than the income from lost farmland." Lewis and Matthiessen revealed that the "farmers were evicted to make room for speculators in lakeside lots." This was a revelation they made before the land was sold, indicating that it had been a plan long before the general public knew.

The article continued, "There will be no electrical generator in the Tellico Dam."

"Industry does not need new lakeside sites for jobs in the area: There are 24 existing major dams and lakes within 60 miles of the Tellico Dam, and most of them have long undeveloped stretches of shoreline. The TVA found that the dam would cost the area more jobs than it would create."

It happened as a gradual awakening, when many within TVA and supporters of the project began to rue the day that the Tellico Dam was conceived because they were beginning to realize that opponents of the project had been right and the proponents wrong about everything they had promised.

While TVA waited for the industry they had promised, nature tried to reclaim the land that surrounded the lake by growing vegetation. Only this time, it wasn't the desirable farmer-grown types of vegetation. Weed seeds had settled on the bulldozed soil and sprouted in abundance, growing rapidly and blocking the lake views of remaining residents who lived in homes within sight of the lake. Some asked TVA for permission to clean these vacant lots. Farmers asked if they could plant crops there while the land remained idle. TVA decided to develop a policy to allow farmers to lease various portions based on bids. Those who wished to use the land had to obtain an agricultural license in order to secure a bid. The most productive acres were leased quickly, some to former owners, some to other farmers.

A rather odd parcel in the Mt. Zion community remained open because it was cornered by a steep bank that was grown up in scrub brush. It did not appear to be suitable for pasture or any agricultural use. Nevertheless, one person did bid on it for $25. He was awarded the lease by TVA after stating on his agricultural license application that he planned to graze a goat and plant a garden on the plot. It was assumed that he would have to build a fence to keep his goat out of his garden. The story and photos of the acreage was printed in the *Monroe County Advocate* on July 23. The story gave the dispirited population a much-needed laugh.

As people in the region waited and saw that nothing new was happening, more and more businesses closed and shuttered their doors. There were no new takers of the vacant properties.

Many of the older long-time residents of Vonore and Loudon were afraid they were going to have to live out their final days in ghost towns because so many people had been forced to move away. There were not enough customers left for the stores to remain open. Some of the people who had moved away were not landowners but people who had worked in the numerous businesses that were dependent on the river or the land. There were no jobs left for them.

EPILOGUE
THE DROWNED VALLEY

1982

It had been three years since the river was impounded, but no development had taken place. Now, more of TVA's backers had begun to realize they had made a mistake. Some of them were now known to lie to newcomers, claiming that they had been against the dam when old timers knew which side of the struggle they had been on.

Embarrassed, TVA proposes to use what was left of the valley as a toxic waste facility. Those plans were made in secret. It is not known whether or not any of the major publications knew of the plans because someone from inside TVA showed the plans to a valley paper. There was a tremendous outcry from the public. Those who had promoted the project were against it.

Inside TVA's big office building in downtown Knoxville, board members and personnel were furious how the story of the toxic waste site had been leaked. They had planned to get the deal sealed between them and government officials before the public had a chance to protest. Who leaked the information? No one knew for sure, but they did realize that it was doubtful if any of the TVA employees from the area would have been keen on the idea of having toxic waste in their backyards. They could even point fingers at each other because some of them planned to remain living in the area. Nevertheless, the uproar gave them a reason to go ahead and lay off the numerous extra people they had hired in promoting the project. Some had already been let go.

Meanwhile, many Loudon businesses were closing because the Davis community had stopped trading in Loudon. It was now much easier and closer for them to drive across the Tellico Dam to Lenoir City via the new Tellico Parkway where the movers and shakers all seemed to push for the destruction of Loudon . It seemed to many that the politicians in Lenoir City really hated Loudon; some said it had been that way since the Civil War because of divided loyalties in that war. As a consequence, Lenoir City had mostly Democrat leaders and Loudon, Republicans. As time passed and new people came into the area, there was change and representation became more bipartisan but old rivalries continued.

Lenoir City now had the greater population and subsequently was in charge with more representatives and greater influence on the various industrial committees set up by TVA supporters who had always promoted the dam and favored industrialization of the entire area.

As John Lackey Jr. put it, "It was the city socialists against the country capitalists." And, in many ways, that did sum up the central issue of the struggle.

April, 1982

The Tennessee Legislature whose members were growing tired of ongoing complaints regarding the aftermath of the Tellico Dam fiasco decided they must do something to help TVA transfer the land it had taken. They created the Tellico Reservoir Development Agency (TRDA) and gave that board the legal authority to develop land inside TVA's taking line. In other words, they created a puppet board so that TVA could do whatever it wanted to do with the land. The TRDA board was to be composed of nine members; three of these would be the County Executives (now called County Mayors) of the three counties, Blount, Loudon, and Monroe. Each mayor would appoint two members to make the total of nine. Ironically, Vonore, the municipality that suffered the greatest losses in land, people, and property, including its high school, was to have no representation on the board. Instead, they elected Tellico Plains Mayor Charles Hall as the first president of the group.

On August 25, 1982, TVA's board approved a contract that transferred 11,000 acres to TRDA, with TVA retaining an equal amount of land for recreational and historical uses.

Although relieved that the toxic waste dump had been defeated, the remaining residents of the valley were understandably nervous about what would happen next. They followed closely the actions taken by the TVA board and the legislature's creation of TRDA. Basically, the Tennessee legislature gave TRDA permission to do whatever it wished to do. It set up no checks whatsoever. Many people buried their heads in the sand and failed to notice TVA's ever-changing tactics, equating the latest transfer of property to the shell-games of carnivals of the past.

One person commented, "Just when the government wants you to believe that TVA is no longer making decisions, you realize that they are still in the driver's seat, only by another name: TRDA." And, it certainly was true, pro-TVA politicians and their appointees, their puppets, were in control of the organization.

It was TRDA's plans to sell the 11,000 acres at auction after the Tennessee legislature gave them authority to do so. When former landowners heard that the land was going to be sold at auction, they began making inquiries, wanting to bid on the land they once owned that was above water but within the taking line.

Jim Graham was a very successful and prosperous farmer who had done well on his new farm located on the French Broad River near Newport. He was a smart, hard-working, well-educated young man who had been making a good living from his agricultural enterprises, but home was home, as he said. He missed his friends in Loudon. His widowed mother had moved to a house in Loudon and his sister lived nearby in Knox County, so it was understandable that he wanted to buy back some of the land in the valley. Mainly, he loved the place he had been forced to leave.

Members of the board got together with some TVA people and wrung their hands.

"I didn't think any of the farmers would be able or willing to bid on this property. What are we going to do if this Graham fellow and some of the others offer the highest bid and want to farm it? We don't want it to be farmed! We've got people who want to develop it and put this place on the map," a Monroe County appointee said.

"There's another reason we can't have them bidding. You know the land is going to go a lot higher than what we paid them, so that would make us look bad, don't you think?" a TVA spokesman said. "We'll just announce that former landowners will not be allowed to bid at the auction, and there is not a damned thing they can do about it." It was true; the state legislature had given them the authority.

Thus, the decision was made. TRDA sold the property to speculators and the media was strangely silent about this additional insult to the landowners, the fact that former landowners were not allowed to bid. Some of them, like Jim Graham for example, could easily have been the high bidder on some of the property at auction although most of the land taken from him was underwater. A portion of the Graham farm can still be seen by the silos which rise like ghostly sentries from the shallow lake.

Many of the speculators resold lots quickly from the land they were able to purchase at the auction, while other developers took more time to ensure even greater profits. Acres and acres of prime and productive soil were paved to create asphalt parking lots. Most buyers didn't care that the land was obtained by force; others simply didn't know.

On the day of the auction, Beryl Moser watched as

his small acreage was auctioned off. It was hard to fathom, but, of all people, a native of North Korea was one of the buyers of his lots.

"There I was shooting at these people in Korea for our government and then the government took my home and land away from me and sold it to one of them." He was talking to Kat and Tish sometime after the sale. He looked down at the hat he was holding in his hand, looking back into the past, still stoic and determined to persevere. It was not surprising that Beryl was well-loved by members of his community, Kat thought, because he had handled his situation as well as any man could.

He kept up with the resale of his land, or what could have been his own lots, now lakefront property on the edge of the new lake, and saw the price escalate to half a million dollars. Imagine, he was paid $12,000 and TVA and the people who purchased it made more than half a million on those five acres!

The Scarecrow was still around and active at random intervals of time. Many believed he had set fire to the first TRDA building which burned to the ground. After the in-your-face treatment of former landowners, vandalism did escalate to more serious events; sugar was poured into the gas tanks of TVA vehicles. No one knew how many incidents could be attributed to the scarecrow or to others, but pictures of the graffiti left by him kept appearing in news articles, but the scarecrow remained free and unknown.

1983

TVA begins a relationship with a major developer, Cooper Communities, based in Arkansas. Together, they decide to allow Cooper to create a high-income, resort-home development. Tellico Village was the name of the community they created. The Village, as it came to be called, offers a Yacht Club, golf course, boat docks and other amenities. Because TVA was in such a hurry to close the gates of the dam back in 1979, they left numerous farm silos standing; these serve as reminders of a farming community that once existed. Often motorboats of various kinds will whiz by the old silos and, occasionally, young people will climb up and dive into the water from them.

1986

The Sequoyah Birthplace Museum was opened on the 65 acre permanent easement given to the Eastern Band of Cherokee by TVA. This was an effort by the TVA to ease the tension between them and the Cherokees following the court's refusal to intervene on behalf of the Native Americans who had tried to preserve their historical homeland and burial sites along the Little Tennessee River which TVA had desecrated before flooding them with a lake.

In addition to the museum, a Memorial burial mound was built on the easement so that the remains of 191 Cherokees could be reinterred there. The first graves of those Native Americans were located on various sites near the 18th century Cherokee towns and villages along the Little Tennessee River. Initially, after having been dug up, the remains were taken to the University of Tennessee and stored in boxes in a basement for years. The uproar from the Cherokees persisted during those years and finally brought action by TVA.

While the burial mound was in the process of being built, a bomb scare occurred. One newspaper attributed the threat to the Scarecrow. This elicited a response from the Scarecrow himself; it was a denial of the bomb threat with an added bit of information, "I like Injuns." It is believed that the scrolled response written with childlike-printed letters was an attempt to deceive and protect his identity and, apparently, he was successful in doing that.

Historians will recall that Sequoyah developed the syllabary, often referred to as the Cherokee alphabet. It is considered a notable achievement, not only for its time, but for its continued significance. Instead of the individual letters which make up the English alphabet and language, the Cherokee letters represent syllables. The museum features the syllabary as a giant graphic along with video and audio so that one, given enough time, could learn the language.

It displays large photographs of some of the archaeological digs, including some which show skeletal remains of ancient Cherokee. It also includes a considerable amount of Cherokee history with exhibits of many arrowheads of various types, diagrams of early buildings, and general information given in the audio of a number of videos located at different areas of the museum.

Written in numerous places throughout the museum is the following statement about Sequoyah (1776-1843): "Never before, or since, in the history of the world has one man, not literate in any language, perfected a system for reading and writing a language."

Twelve miles southeast of the Sequoyah Museum is another place cherished by the Cherokee, the Tanasi Memorial which marks the site of the Cherokee village from which the state of Tennessee got its name.

TVA transferred some of the acreage that was adjacent to the old Fort Loudoun, built in 1756, to the state in the form of an 853-acre day use park with picnic tables and some boat ramps; also a campground and swimming area are not too far away. Locals who began swimming in the newly created lake noted that the water was at first cold and relatively clear, similar to how the water felt in the Little T, but within a not-so-very-long time span, it became tepid and pretty much like many of the other of TVA lakes, rather dirty.

When initiating the project, TVA planned to flood the old fort in spite of the fact that it was often visited by school children as part of their study of history. Fort Loudoun was the first Anglo-Saxon structure constructed west of the Alleghenies, built by the British during the French and Indian War (1754-1763). It had deteriorated through the years and was reconstructed during the Great Depression and designated a National Landmark in 1965. The late Alice Milton worked fervently to save the fort from being flooded. TVA finally agreed to move it, but historians said that would destroy its historical significance. In the end, TVA decided to raise it so that it would be above the lake. They used tremendous amounts of fill dirt and built up the land in order to replace the structure on the same location. Now, instead of seeing the river running by, one sees a lake on two sides. The foundation markers of the blockhouse which was used by the fort is now across a finger of the lake and accessed by a separate road.

A few light industries finally located along the relocated Highway 72 which now runs between the Highway 411 and 11. The operations there use mainly temporary workers and pay them much less than other industries in the area. There are office buildings there too, for example, the headquarters of the TRDA; also a credit union, that sort of thing, nothing that was promised by TVA and Charles Hall. Some joke about the fact that no one from Vonore comes to Loudon anymore, fondly repeating the old saying, "You can't get there from here anymore." It is true; one has to drive around the lake to access any road to connect the two municipalities.

Prior to the new lake which flooded the old road, although curvy, it had linked Vonore to Loudon. Residents of the Davis community also used that road to come to Loudon to trade.

Although residents of Tellico Village share an address with the people of Loudon, they, for the most part, do not shop in Loudon. They have their own retail outlets and grocery stores and restaurants. In fact, acres of the once productive soils of the Davis, Ritchey and other once productive farms are now covered in asphalt for huge parking lots outside their retail shops and banks and gas stations. A nursing home is located on a spot where one farmhouse stood.

The Village has certainly grown with residents migrating from numerous places, primarily from North. They now have their own commissioner on the Loudon County Commission. In addition to bringing themselves to the South, to Tennessee, some in the Village brought with them their former values about government. As a consequence, taxes have continued to rise in Loudon County.

Following his victory in getting the Tellico Dam built, Charles Hall, the politically popular Democrat mayor of Tellico Plains lobbied successfully for the construction of the Cherohala Skyway which linked his town with Robbinsville, North Carolina. Although he had previously scoffed at suggestions that he promote tourism in his picturesque town instead of industry near the Tellico Dam, miles from where he lived, he must have had a change of attitude in the 80's. As far as anyone knows, he never apologized for his advocacy for the dam, but he did, nevertheless, become interested in the new tourist-driven small businesses that discovered Tellico Plains on their way to see Bald River Falls and the Trout Fishery located in the Cherokee National Forest. Hall who owned and operated the Tellico Telephone Company from 1954 until 1985 is said to have "gotten rich on TVA propaganda," mostly from rural development grants to relocate phone lines as a result of the dam project. He certainly relished his fame because he created a museum in Tellico Plains which he named after himself, the Charles Hall Museum. There, old telephone equipment and other antique items are displayed.

1997

The Tennessee Legislature named the bridge over Laurel Branch on the Cherohala Skyway "The Charles Hall Bridge." Soon after, the state learned that the once popular mayor was not so popular anymore, at least not with everyone, because the sign was shot to pieces time and time again. The State finally told the family that they could not afford to keep replacing the sign on the bridge and if they wanted it there, they would have to maintain it themselves.

Following the development of Tellico Village, other upscale communities were created from land taken from Tennesseans by TVA. More and more tracts of land were sold by TDRA for upscale residential communities. For example, not far from Tellico Village, Rariety Bay was created. As part of the draw to sell people properties in the Rarity Bay community, an equestrian center was established, complete with a barn, show ring, white-fenced pastures, and a replica of a famous bronze Remington statue. It was quite enticing to horse lovers who could afford it. Unfortunately for some of them, as soon as the lots were all sold, so was the facility. In private hands, the stall rent of $600 a month is more than many can afford to pay. A more recent community in the Vonore area is Kahite, with another golf course, boat docks and other desirable amenities afforded by the well-to-do residents.

As one might expect, newcomers to the area are a mixed bag of types . . . as varied as people everywhere, some good, some bad, some nice and some described as down-right hateful, smug, know-it-alls. The people in this later group are known as "damn Yankees" followed by the old joke: Question: "You know what a damn-Yankee is? Answer: Someone who comes down from the North for a visit and stays!"

A few individuals from the Village have shown an interest in the pretty little river town of Loudon. They have opened shops and art galleries, joining with some of the locals in an effort to revitalize the town known for having a beautiful old Courthouse that is on the National Register of Historic Places.

2017

Now in his 80's, Beryl Moser is no longer a bachelor. He continues to be City Judge of Vonore, having been reelected during every election. He still stands straight and remains committed and as proud as ever of the timeless values about what is right and what is wrong.

According to Edna Blankenship, a longtime resident of Vonore who serves as a resident historian in the Museum there, Beryl is loved and respected by everyone because he is just and fair as a City Judge.

"His counsel is so wise." Edna said, explaining how Moser has had a positive influence on the lives of many young people whose mischief and misdeeds landed them in front of him.

"I think it has a lasting effect on them, I really do. And, Beryl is not paid. He does the job out of the kindness of his heart and the needs of our community."

Today in 2017, the head of TVA makes a salary of six and a half million dollars, according to Congressman Jimmy Duncan who differs somewhat from his late father's views about the land taken by TVA.

After TVA obtained Beryl Moser's property which including a home, outbuildings and five acres through the law of eminent domain for $12,800, he refused to take the check for eight years.

Quite agile for his age, Moser served as a referee for football and basketball games for 62 years, not retiring from that job until he reached 80, becoming the oldest referee ever in the state and still able to run up and down the field or basketball court to keep up with the action of the young players.

Today, Judge Moser continues to appear much as he did nearly 38 years ago as a younger man standing on his front porch, waiting for the federal marshals to usher him away. He will still look you straight in the eye and repeat what he said then, "To hell with TVA."

In many ways, Beryl Moser is an example of the kind of people who couldn't be fooled when President Abraham Lincoln made his now famous statement:

"You can fool some of the people all of the time,
And all of the people some of the time,
But you can't fool all of the people all of the time."

Abraham Lincoln

NOTES FROM THE AUTHOR

I first learned about the Tellico Project from my father, the late Ben B. Simpson, who was against it from the beginning. I also knew many of the families who were displaced; some were members of my church.

Later, as the long struggle and years went by, I understood why most thinking people opposed the project so I wrote letters to the various newspapers. Later, after I became a journalist, I covered many of the events which transpired. So, in order to tell the story of what happened here, I had some of the fictional characters walk and talk in my shoes, seeing what I saw and interacting with real individuals who were involved.

I camped out with the Cherokee during their peaceful protest at Chota, talked to the many people who were there saying goodbye to that historic place.

I was very pleased to learn that a letter I had written to a Knoxville newspaper was clipped out and mailed to CBS by Alfred Davis, president of the Landowners Association and that it caught the attention of one of their producers, Al Wasserman, with their "60 Minutes" program. I was honored that Mr. Wasserman looked me up when he and his crew came here, shook my hand and said, "That was quite a letter you wrote."

I was with Davis and the CBS crew when we sneaked through the woods to film the eviction of 85-

year old Nellie McCall as described by characters in the novel.

In those days, I had much more respect for the national media than I have today. Although never perfect, the national media was, in my opinion, more ethical and more honest than it is today. Still, they were remiss in their coverage of the lawsuit, seeming to delight in making fun of a little fish for stopping a big government project. They missed all the other significant underlying issues until after the death of the river. Then, they printed some significant observations when it was too late.

I was privileged to be inside the homes of both Nellie McCall and Beryl Moser, along with numerous other members of the media as they waited for the federal marshals to come and evict them from their homes. It was indeed a moving experience. Many of us who live here did not own any of the taken land, but we loved the river and the valley and referred to it as ours.

There were other protests that I did not cover in this novel, including numerous parades. One was a tractor brigade through downtown Knoxville, an attempt to draw attention to the significant agricultural industry in the area.

The Cherokee camp-out at Chota was nothing like the demonstrations and protests of today. They were very reverent and peaceful in displaying their wishes of saving the river and its valley. Although it may not be possible, I wish the newcomers, especially the wealthy people now living in the upscale communities in the three affected counties, Blount, Monroe and

Loudon, would understand and respect the value of what was here before them and help us share our story to perhaps save lands that might be threatened in the future. Hopefully, TVA has or will reexamine its purpose and methods. Once upon a time, we called our country a "sweet land of liberty."

It is my fervent hope that Tennessee history taught to our children will reflect the truth about TVA's land grab and the flooding of some of the richest farming soil in this part of the country; that it was simply a make-work project for TVA.

How sweet was my valley.

The photo below was taken in the 1940's on what was the William A. Graham's River View Farm now buried under Tellico Lake. Their old silos, shown on the back cover, remain. Below, Mr. "Bill" is shown with his son Jim who later became one of the state's most outstanding farmers and agricultural leaders.

William A. Graham and his son, James R. Graham River View Farm Little T River Late 1940s

Photo of a Family Photo

When Jim was a grown man and prosperous farmer, he heard that TRDA was going to auction some of the dry land that TVA took. He wanted to bid on some of it, but the TRDA refused to let him. None of the former owners whose land was taken by TVA under the law of Eminent Domain were allowed to bid.

Photo shared by Julie Graham Walker.

These photos show some of the property formerly owned by the late Col. Charles Bacon. He generated his own electricity before TVA was created.

Photos shared by the Amburn family.

John Hair, Vice-Chief of the Keetoowah Band of Cherokee in Tahlequah, Oklahoma, had heard stories passed down by his ancestors about the trail of tears from their former homeland along the Little Tennessee River, but he had never seen the place. A professional airline pilot, he had always planned to visit and realized that the October 20, 1979, protest would probably be the last chance he would have.

Photo by David Smiley.

Ollie Otter, Loyd Sequoyah, shown above, and left to right below, Rhonda Cucumber and Echo White Deer, traveled from Cherokee, N.C. to protest the flooding of the Cherokee's ancestral capital and burial mounds along the Little T. *Photos by David Smiley.*

Fort Loudoun is shown as it looks today, 17 ft. higher than it was before TVA took it down and filled in the area to prevent it from being covered by water after they damned the Little Tennessee River. The lake can be seen in the distance where the river once flowed.

Originally built in 1756, it was one of the earliest British fortifications on what was then the western frontier. It was designated as a National Historic Landmark in 1965, about the same time Congress appropriated funds for the Tellico Project.

Photo by Ron Bivens.

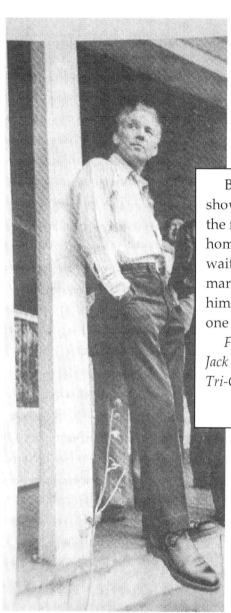

Beryl Moser is shown standing on the front porch of his home amid reporters waiting for federal marshals to evict him. He was the last one out.

From a photo by Jack Waters for the Tri-County Observer.

ABOUT THE AUTHOR

Sarah Simpson Bivens is a native and resident of Loudon, Tennessee. As a journalist, she won numerous first-place awards for work published in the *Tri-County Observer* and *Southline Magazine* . Later, she and her husband Ron Bivens co-edited and published *The Loudon County Independent.*

In 2015, her first novel, *Crazy Creek,* a highly rated work of fiction, was published. Two years later, her second novel *How Sweet Was My Valley*, based on the true story of historical events, was completed. Both books are set in the mountains and valleys of the East Tennessee area where she lives and writes.

She and her husband live on a family farm which they share with five horses, two dogs, eight cats, and wildlife.